Collaborations for Social Justice

Collaborations for Social Justice

Professionals, Publics, and Policy Change

Edited by Andrew L. Barlow

ROWMAN & LITTLEFIELD PUBLISHERS, INC.
Lanham • Boulder • New York • Toronto • Plymouth, UK

ROWMAN & LITTLEFIELD PUBLISHERS, INC.

Published in the United States of America
by Rowman & Littlefield Publishers, Inc.
A wholly owned subsidiary of The Rowman & Littlefield Publishing Group, Inc.
4501 Forbes Boulevard, Suite 200, Lanham, Maryland 20706
www.rowmanlittlefield.com

Estover Road
Plymouth PL6 7PY
United Kingdom

British Library Cataloguing in Publication Information Available

Library of Congress Cataloging-in-Publication Data

Collaborations for social justice : professionals, publics, and policy change / edited by
Andrew L. Barlow.
    p. cm.
  ISBN-10: 0-7425-5931-9 (cloth : alk. paper)
  ISBN-13: 978-0-7425-5931-8 (cloth : alk. paper)
  ISBN-10: 0-7425-5932-7 (pbk. : alk. paper)
  ISBN-13: 978-0-7425-5932-5 (pbk. : alk. paper)
  1. Community power—United States. 2. Social advocacy—United States. 3.
Professional employees—United States—Political activity. I. Barlow, Andrew L., 1948–

  HM776.A38 2007
  307.1'40973—dc22   2007010933

Printed in the United States of America

∞™ The paper used in this publication meets the minimum requirements of
American National Standard for Information Sciences—Permanence of Paper
for Printed Library Materials, ANSI/NISO Z39.48-1992.

Contents

~

Introduction

The idea for this book arose out of two specific events. The first was a unique conference that took place at Stanford University in October 2003. The conference brought together academics, journalists, civil rights lawyers, and community organizers to discuss the potential impact of banning racial data and what could be done to defend the collection of such data.[1] The discussion took place in the final week before a California election in which Proposition 54 was on the ballot. This ballot initiative proposed to amend the state constitution to prohibit state agencies from collecting or keeping data about race. Most of the five hundred or so conference participants were active in the ultimately successful campaign to defeat it. The conference was, by all accounts, a remarkable success. All of the presentations and discussions were tightly focused on a single theme that was defined by the Prop. 54 campaign, and each added new dimensions to the participants' understanding of race and racism in the United States.[2] The conference demonstrated beyond any doubt the power of political practice rooted in the defense of civil rights to magnify the quality of academics' research and writing. The remarkable cross-fertilization of work from many different disciplines, held together by the glue of a political campaign, sparked a new interest in creating ongoing collaborations between community-based activists and researchers, lawyers, and journalists.

The second event that gave impetus to this book was the 2004 Annual Meeting of the American Sociological Association (ASA). At the meeting's sessions, ASA president Michael Burawoy organized a wide-ranging discussion of the value of public sociology, by which he meant the dissemination of, and engagement with, sociological ways of thinking among broad publics. Many of these discussions focused on the need to create bridges between academic research and publics comprised of people who are socially marginalized. The ASA established a Task Force on the Institutionalization of Public Sociology to initiate ongoing support for such collaborative work within the discipline.[3]

The selection of authors for this book was an easy task: many of them have worked over the years with other contributors to this volume in political campaigns or in other collaborations to influence public opinion. It is therefore not incidental that all of the authors in this volume work and live in California. The editor, in particular, has long admired the other contributors' sophisticated understanding of the relationship between academic and political work. The long-standing ties between many of the authors explain the ease with which we could weave a common set of issues and a common language into each chapter. We speak a similar language because we approach our professional work in similar ways.

There are some fundamental principles that underscore all the contributions to this volume. First, we share a commitment to democracy, by which we mean the creation of social arrangements that are inclusive of all people regardless of class, race, nationality, ethnicity, gender, or sexual orientation. Second, we share the understanding that everyone, not just the socially recognized "experts," is capable of developing ideas. Third, we share an understanding that people's ideas are shaped by their location in society. Those who are located in marginal positions in society are particularly capable of thinking critically and insightfully about social problems, as well as their own situations. Fourth, we share an understanding of the dimension of power in intellectual work, and we understand that the mobilization of power by those who are marginalized or outright excluded from the existing social order is of vital importance to advance ideas that flow from their experience. Finally, we share a belief that professionals can and do play important roles in facilitating the emergence of ideas from marginalized communities and that the mobilization of community-based power ("from below") is necessary to make these ideas historically significant.

This book is a collective process of reflection on our own practices, done in the hope of calling others to the tasks of professionals doing community empowerment work. We sincerely hope that the accounts of our efforts will demonstrate two basic principles: that the democratization of research and specialized practice enables the production of new insights, and that professionals' participation in the process of empowerment of low-income communities is transformative in ways that are enriching both professionally and personally.

Most of all, this book is dedicated to students who are contemplating careers as professionals, in the hopes that by reading these accounts they might contemplate a different path in the search for meaningful work.

Notes

1. Conference organizers included professors Troy Duster (NYU), David Wellman (UCSC), Andrew Barlow (UCB and DVC), Claude Steele (Stanford), the late George Fredrickson (Stanford), and Hazel Markus (Stanford); attorneys Eva Patterson and Susan Serrano (Equal Justice Society); and journalists Steve Monteil (Annenberg Center for Justice and Journalism) and Elaine Elinson (Equal Justice Society).

2. Video excerpts from the conference are available on the Equal Justice Society website, www.equaljusticesociety.org/research.html.

3. Andrew Barlow is a member of this task force.

~

CHAPTER ONE

Transformative Collaborations: Professionals and Minority Community Power

Andrew L. Barlow

The quest for social justice is a significant and permanent feature of political life in the United States, as in virtually all societies in this era.[1] The late twentieth century in particular witnessed the emergence of protest politics on a growing number of issues, involving collective action aimed at altering the distribution of resources or even the basic structure of societies. This heightened demand for social justice, necessitated by oppressive social conditions, was also enabled by the expanding role of the state, which opened up many new avenues for marginalized people to politically mobilize for equality and recognition of their dignity. Today, even as the role of government is being fundamentally altered in ways that are detrimental to underprivileged people, millions of people in the United States continue to confront and work to overcome various forms of discrimination and exploitation.

While social justice advocates have many different agendas, they generally agree on the fundamental need for the more equitable distribution of social resources on a wide variety of issues, ranging from education to health care to employment to housing to retirement benefits. The widespread and tenacious advocacy for social justice, especially given the growing use today of repressive state power against people of color and poor people generally at home and around the world, is living proof of Martin Luther King's belief that the quest for social justice is a timeless expression of people's longing for human dignity and connections to one another.[2] The permanence of social

1

justice advocacy also vividly demonstrates advocates' understanding of Frederick Douglass's immortal words: "Power concedes nothing without a demand. It never did and it never will."

The quest for social justice today is anything but simple. To accomplish any meaningful goal, social justice advocates must develop the capacity to formulate, influence, and implement government policies. Often, the policy questions are complex and highly technical issues, requiring advocates to master specialized skills. And, just as important, advocates must master the art of politics, seeking the most effective ways to bring pressure to bear on government agencies and corporations. Social justice advocacy thus requires far more than protest politics—it requires the acquisition of considerable knowledge, power, and access to institutionalized resources.

Over the past forty years, many social justice advocates have acquired more sophisticated skills and far greater expertise, as well as far greater access to positions of power and influence, than at any time in the past. A generation of activists from the movements of the 1960s and 1970s has acquired the credentials, skills, and positioning necessary to be effective "insiders." Today, an unknown number of people—certainly in the hundreds of thousands—in the United States with social justice agendas and values occupy positions in government, education, health care, and other public institutions, as well as within the private sector. Among the most visible advocates are those who have attained political office, exemplified by Congressman John Lewis, a former president of the Student Nonviolent Coordinating Committee. These advocates are often quite adept at using the power and resources of their institutional position to advance social justice agendas and have been able to effect significant redistributions of funding and other resources in the process.

However, the institutionalization of social justice advocacy is not just a success story. At the same time that social justice advocates have achieved a historically unprecedented level of institutional positioning, the changing role of the state in American society—and, indeed, in all of the developed countries—is eroding the social justice achievements of the past. A generation ago, when social justice advocates were likely to be outside institutions protesting, rather than inside making policies, the welfare state model was in full play. Political elites in the 1950s and 1970s seized the opportunities presented by the rapid expansion of the U.S. economy and state to practice what Krieger terms a "growth coalition" approach to governance.[3] In this model, politicians intervened in social conflicts (such as the movement against societal racism) with new laws and public funding aimed at appeasing all sides in the conflict and, not incidentally, expanding state power. In the welfare state era, embracing social justice politics could be, and often was, also an effective way for politicians to amass personal power.[4]

But today, the role of government in society is changed. Rather than actively intervening in and mitigating social conflicts, government today is primarily concerned with fostering the private accumulation of wealth.[5] The last thirty years have also been marked by slow economic growth and the most rapid increase in income and wealth inequality in U.S. history.[6] Rather than greeting social protest as an opportunity to expand entitlement programs and civil rights, politicians today are far more likely to view social justice demands as dangerous and illegitimate incursions on property rights.[7]

Social justice advocates who are well positioned in institutions of power today thus often face a paradoxical situation. On the one hand, they enjoy a degree of access to power and funding of which activists a generation ago could only dream. On the other hand, however, the government's disinvestment in public education, public health care, public services, and entitlement programs for the poor; the lack of enforcement of civil rights; growing inequality; and economic stagnation are eroding the living standards of an increasing number of people in the United States, especially poor people of color.[8] As social justice advocates working inside government agencies or corporate offices attempt to remedy increasingly dire social problems, they face increasingly stringent fiscal, legal, and policy restrictions on what they can do.

These trends have also significantly eroded grassroots social justice organizations' access to funding and political influence, especially those in poor, minority communities. Nonetheless, despite the lack of governmental or corporate support, and often isolated from professionals, community-based groups are today engaged in a wide array of social justice activities, ranging from labor organizing among immigrant workers, to youth violence reduction efforts by black churches, to demands for educational reform by Latino and Asian parents and students, to voter registration drives among new citizens. Community-based social justice organizations persist, and new ones appear every day, despite the increasingly adverse situation they have faced for the past twenty-five years. Simply put, these groups exist because they have to. But the decline in public and private funding, increasing social inequality, as well as the growing hostility of government and corporations to their demands, all certainly challenge their ability to effect political and economic reforms today.

Another casualty of this era is an important group of nonprofit organizations that can be described as professional social justice advocacy organizations. This type of social justice organization consists mainly of a professional staff that advocates for a specific issue or an abstract "community" (e.g., "the environment," "disabled community," "women's community," "GLTBQ community"). Often, professional advocacy organizations for such abstract causes are memberless groups situated in Washington, D.C., where paid staff members engage in lobbying, policy advocacy, and fund-raising. Some advocacy organizations do have members, but the purpose of membership in many such groups is to support the work of the professional staff. Both memberless and membership professional advocacy organizations often have only the most abstract connection to the people they claim to represent. As Skocpol observes:

> The United States today has the most pluralist polity in the world, yet associations claiming to speak for the people lack incentives and capacities to mobilize large numbers of people through direct personal contacts and on-going involvement in interactive settings. Yawning gaps have emerged between local voluntary efforts and the professional advocates and grant makers who seek national influence.[9]

The quest for social justice in the United States, then, continues to be very active but is, as a rule, strangely deformed, with a "yawning gap" between those who have access to political influence, expertise, and funding on the one hand and the community-based associations seeking to organize and mobilize people on their own behalf on the other.[10]

Situated in this context, the questions that this book seeks to answer can now be posed: What happens when professionals realize that their institutional authority and certified expertise are not sufficient to alter the ability of marginalized people to make claims on the increasingly unequally distributed resources of society? What do lawyers do when they find that the space left by court decisions to articulate a legal argument in support of school desegregation is too narrow to make a significant difference in the long struggle for racial justice in education? What do health providers do if they decide that environmental toxins or the increasing lack of access to health care for people of color is making people sick more than any germ or virus? What do educators do if they find that more than outcomes testing is needed to stem the high dropout rates of black and Latino students? If and when policy options and resources dwindle, and when government becomes increasingly indifferent—and even hostile—to the needs of marginal people, and when the needs of people for professional services seem bottomless, what should professionals who care about social justice do?

Conversely, what should community-based social justice advocates do about their shrinking access to institutional resources and government power? How can they increase their capacity to significantly impact policy and funding decisions on issues that affect their communities at a time of growing government hostility to social justice issues? The answer to these questions, we believe, lies in the development of a sophisticated notion of collaborative social justice work, based on community empowerment in which professionals play an integral part.

The Resurgence of Social Justice Professionalism Today

It is remarkable, given the growing governmental antipathy to social justice, that a new spirit of public engagement is animating professional organizations in the United States. The 2004 and 2005 annual meetings of the American Sociological Association (ASA) were devoted to wide-ranging explorations of the tasks of "public sociology."[11] Other professional associations, such as the American Economics Association, the American Public Health Association, and the National Educational Association, regularly discuss the efforts of professionals to promote public policy and public empowerment agendas. The ASA, the American History Association, and an influential group of American anthropologists have launched websites to promote professional engagement with public issues.[12] Numerous groups of academics, lawyers, health professionals, educators, and journalists are seeking new ways to participate in public discussion and political action. Some multidisciplinary groups are forming "think tanks" to promote public policies that advance social justice.[13] Some are engaging in electoral politics.[14] Others collaborate on legal briefs.[15] Others are working with community-based nonprofit organizations, seeking to make them more effective advocates for social justice issues.[16]

This new interest in professional engagement with "publics" is motivated by several different professional interests. Public professionalism is, in part, a response to religious fundamentalists' attacks on professional claims to scientifically based authority on a wide variety of fronts, ranging from biology to psychiatry to sociology. These attacks, which include government officials blocking the collection and dissemination of scientific data and their refusal to fund scientific studies deemed unacceptable to Christian fundamentalists, have forced many professionals who had previously prided themselves on their apolitical "objectivity" to reconsider their positions.[17] Second, a long-term concern motivating public engagement by social scientists is the belief that social science must counteract a dangerous trend toward social disengagement, a loss of civic consciousness, and a shrinking of Americans' ideas about the world. This interest has motivated some of the classic works of American social science, including the writings of Lewis Mumford and

Robert Bellah.[18] And, finally, public professionalism is at times motivated by the radical stance first pronounced by Karl Marx but also embraced by non-Marxists such as C. Wright Mills and Paolo Freire: the purpose of intellectual activity is not to understand the world but to change it, in a process initiated and led by oppressed and exploited peoples.

The engagement of professionals with "publics" thus is motivated by a complex mix of factors: the defense of scientific expertise, the defense of professional authority, efforts to participate in the revival of "civil society" (understood here as the many ways people develop social ties and culture outside the realm of the state and corporate arrangements), and a call for the reengagement of marginalized publics with the state.[19] The arguments made for these different modes of professional engagement with "publics" are thus very different.[20] But for one or even all of these reasons, interest in public engagement is growing in all knowledge-based professions, as all—including the natural sciences—can and do address matters of political and moral concern to various publics. But there are many publics, and there are different ways that professionals can engage with them.

One way that public professional activity can be delineated is by its *mode of engagement* with a public. Traditional public professional activity—by far the predominant mode—is unidirectional, entailing the issuing of proclamations to the public by people claiming professional expertise on matters of public concern. But public professionalism can also be multidirectional, as professionals not only seek to impart expertise to publics but take the experiences, activities, and knowledge of a lay public as important factors in the development of professional knowledge and activities. As we shall see in this volume, this multidirectional conception of the development of knowledge can yield powerful new ideas in fields as disparate as public health, law, and sociology.

Another important distinction among public professional activities is *the type of public* to which professionals relate. Traditional professionals generally take existing societal arrangements as their subject and engage either supportively or critically with the dominant social issues, norms, and behaviors of their time. The great bulk of classic public social science of the mid-twentieth century, for example, took a critical stance toward the institutions and culture of the mass middle-class social order. The "public" that is being engaged by this type of professionalism is a group of people that defines itself in the context of concepts that often emanate from powerful institutions and elites. Because this type of public is one that consumes ideas created by a top-down process of governmental and corporate policies and actions, this grouping is typically a passive and abstract public that affords people very little opportunity to develop their own meanings and social connections.[21]

The other type of public with which professionals engage can be termed grassroots publics. These publics are networks of people seeking to mobilize resources outside the realm of institutionalized, "state," or corporate power to fulfill social needs. Grassroots publics are at times organized around community-based institutions, such as churches, labor unions, and benevolent organizations.[22] They can also be organized through the more informal social connections forged in ethnic and other marginalized communities.[23] The abstract term often used to describe grassroots publics—*community*—is far too vague to capture the overlapping social networks, institutions, and cultural boundaries of real groups of people. Unlike dominant notions of publics created by elites, these networks often become a "public" when they engage in protest activities that make specific claims widely known beyond the group. Thus, grassroots publics are created when networks of people marginalized from "official power" advocate for themselves, defining their problems and making claims on the state or corporations for specific remedies. The very existence of community, for marginalized people, is bound up with the ability of people to demand social justice.

Within the broad conceptualization of public intellectual activity, then, social justice professionalism can be understood as a specific type of professional engagement with people whose structural position in society and their civic consciousness entail opposition and resistance to dominant social arrangements. Social justice professionalism, then, cannot be defined solely by its advocacy for grassroots publics but must also be defined by its multidirectional engagement with that public.

Traditional public professionals (especially social scientists and human service providers) have a long history of advocating for marginalized and oppressed peoples. Many of the social science professions were founded with the vision of social service for such marginalized publics at the core of their mission. And, in all social service-oriented professions, the desire to serve such publics is a powerful motivating force, especially articulated by students preparing to enter these professions. The mode of engagement sought by most professionals advocating for marginalized people is one that can be described as that of a judo expert: the professional intervenes in a fight over public policy and weighs in on the side more favorable to marginalized peoples using their own claims of expertise to make their case. A good example can be found in Duncan Kennedy's description of first-year law students' motivation to seek a law degree:

> A surprisingly large number of law students go to law school with the notion that being a lawyer means something more, something more socially constructive

than just doing a highly respectable job. There is the idea of playing a role an earlier generation associated with Brandeis: the role of service through law, carried out with superb technical competence and also with a deep belief that in its essence law is a progressive force, however much it may be distorted by the actual arrangements of capitalism. There is a contrasting, more radical notion that law is a tool of established interests, that it is in essence super-structural, but that it is a tool that a coldly effective professional can sometimes turn against the dominators. Whereas in the first notion the student aspires to help the oppressed and transform society by bringing out the latent content of a valid ideal, in the second the student sees herself as part technician, part judo expert, able to turn the tables exactly because she never lets herself be mystified by the rhetoric that is so important to other students.[24]

Despite their advocacy of social justice, both of these visions of law and public service maintain traditional professional claims of expertise and power in relationship with passive clients. Both visions—of lawyer as advocate of an ideal and lawyer as a judo expert—presume that the lawyer possesses the expertise and authority necessary to remedy (at least at times) oppressed people's social problems. While not explicitly stated, this kind of professional social justice advocacy can also be—and often is—an entrepreneurial activity, in which professionals seek to gain power and status for themselves by advocating for abstract and silenced publics. Social justice professionalism, then, turns on both the type of public and the type of relationship established with that public. It is to a different type of engagement, often termed "community empowerment" that we now turn.

Community Empowerment

Those practicing community empowerment offer a distinct orientation for social justice advocacy. The process of community empowerment moves the center of decision making and action out from institutionalized power (government, corporations, professional advocacy groups) and into the hands of people who are isolated from, and indeed are often oppressed by, those institutions. Community empowerment places the questions of strategy—naming the problem, identifying the source(s) of the problem, and fashioning a remedy—into the hands of the people experiencing the problem.[25] It also places responsibility for deciding the means (i.e., tactics) to achieve that strategy in the hands of those people. Community empowerment embraces a theory of knowledge, dating back to Marx's ideas of praxis, which acknowledges that those who experience social problems are able to think about and act on these problems in ways that are informed by that experience. But, as Warren and others have noted, community empowerment does not presume that people who experience oppressive conditions therefore automatically have the preexisting capacity to develop strategy and tactics. Community empowerment requires close attention to leadership development: training people embedded in a social network to organize community members and to engage them in a process to identify and mobilize around strategic demands and tactics. Community empowerment presumes the *potential* power of community. This assumption may be more or less realized in any given situation. For community empowerment to have real meaning, people must develop a shared sense of common interest, bound together with shared culture and a common set of social networks. It is wise, especially given the tendency of professionals to claim to represent abstract "communities," to remember Eric Hobsbawm's warning: "[N]ever was the word "community" used more indiscriminately and emptily than in the decades when communities in the sociological sense became hard to find."[26]

Community, for marginalized people, is no abstraction: it is a type of social group, with boundaries and content.[27] Community is not and cannot be created out of thin air: it typically is the creation of complex social processes spanning generations. Without networks and a shared culture, marginalized people are certainly unable to mobilize power in the ways that advocates of community empowerment envision. As Warren observes, community empowerment advocacy often includes efforts to foster community ties. But the presence of objective social conditions supporting a sense of affinity is essential for community to exist. In particular, community formation is most likely to occur among people who understand that they are subjected to societal injustices. For, it is in these conditions—that is, the denial of access to political power, economic opportunity, and social services, especially if they persist for generations—that people seek to create their own networks of self-help and a culture of resistance to salvage their own dignity.[28]

For this reason, especially in the United States, the conditions that make people "ethnic" foster communities that have typically had far greater potential as sites for community empowerment strategies than other types of communities. As Espiritu shows, ethnic communities form through a dual process: first, by experiencing oppression (i.e., racism, national or religious marginalization), and then through a process of self-determination, that is, the development of shared culture and community ties. For example, the slave system imposed racial categorization on people who were enslaved (i.e., by making them "Negroes"), but only those people who were enslaved could create African American ethnicity. Of course, once created, ethnic community resources are used not only to resist the specific problems of racial or national discrimination. Ethnic community ties can be important assets in a wide range of organizing efforts, such as the ways local Mexican networks were mobilized during the Justice for Janitors labor organizing campaign in Los Angeles.[29]

Of course, people in positions of marginality who are not reacting to racism or national or religious oppression also can create community ties. Certainly, the oppression of gays and lesbians has fostered the formation of gay communities. But these communities are bounded and fractured by race, class, and gender differences. Thus, the "gay community" often consists of networks of wealthy white men, but one that excludes gay men of color and women of all races.[30] As well, active labor struggles can create a sense of commonality among workers and their families, but these labor networks are (with some exceptions, often among ethnic minorities) not defined as community-based but as class-based ties. In the context of the United States, then, ethnicity often provides the basis for the most complete and longest lasting kind of community, one that includes people of different classes, genders, and sexual orientations, and one that often shares a common geographic base and long-standing institutional and cultural ties. Other kinds of communities, in contrast, tend to be far more fragmented on class, race, gender, and sexual orientation lines. For this reason, community empowerment strategies are likeliest to succeed when they are rooted in ethnic communities. The lack of clarity over the distinction between ethnic communities and other types of geographic communities may become a serious problem with "regionalist" organizing efforts that may seek to include many white as well as ethnic communities. The potential problem with this approach is that building unity among diverse constituencies may pressure organizers to avoid divisive issues, which can lead regional organizations to have great difficulty addressing issues of racism and the particular problems facing ethnic communities.

There is a long tradition, dating back to the work of Saul Alinsky in the 1940s, to view community empowerment as an end unto itself. In the Alinsky model, the community organizer's mission is to facilitate a process of bringing people together, initiate "bottom-up" leadership training, and then to step out of the process. The content of organizing—decisions about strategy and tactics—must be left to the community-based organization. In Alinsky's model, community empowerment is the goal to be attained because of the belief that "genuine" expressions of community interests are always valid. This notion of the moral validity of "bottom up" decision making in particular fosters a great deal of cynicism about professionals' involvement in community empowerment efforts. As Harry Boyte puts it, "A distinctive feature of the broad citizens groups is to conceptualize the process of deprofessionalization in explicitly . . . political ways."[31] In the Alinsky tradition, professionals (those with institutional authority and power) can be expected to view their own expertise, skills, and knowledge as superior to that of lay community members. Professionals, from this point of view, are likely to dominate and stifle the voices of community members, imposing their own political agendas and tactics on (silenced) community organizations. This view of professional involvement has shaped much of the literature on social movements, where very little attention is given to the potentially constructive collaboration of professional advocates for social justice with community-based social justice movements. Instead, most of the discussions of this issue emphasize the ways professionals co-opt social justice organizations and prevent people without institutional power from being effective community organizers or advocates for their own interests.[32]

In this volume, the authors understand community empowerment as an orientation rather than a strategy. Community empowerment is not an end but a *means* to mobilize people to engage in political action.[33] Political strategy refers to the goals of political mobilization; community empowerment is not a strategic goal but a set of tactical principles—one set of tools among many—to mobilize the power needed to advance political strategies. The valid and crucial premise of community empowerment is that the power to address fundamental social problems must come from outside the institutionalized power arrangements of American society (broadly speaking, "the state"), and that those people who are marginalized, oppressed, and exploited by the existing power structure are likeliest to have the interest in and the capacity to successfully act for change. As well, the community empowerment orientation is rooted in the belief that institutionalized power (and knowledge) is not by itself capable of resolving the fundamental problems of poor, marginalized, and oppressed people. As Anamaria Loya puts it in chapter 2 of this volume, the motivation for lawyers' community empowerment efforts begins with the observation that justice cannot be accomplished within the law. Similarly, Renée et al. (chapter 3) argue that community organizing is essential to effectively develop and promote educational equity agendas, and Pastor et al. (chapter 4) make a similar argument for environmental justice. Social justice, in this view, requires the people who are themselves marginalized and oppressed to challenge the existing parameters of legal processes and public policy from outside the institutionalized parameters of legal power and authority.

The community empowerment orientation also recognizes that people in marginalized communities are capable of thinking about their own situations; intellectual work is not solely the provenance of professionals. For this reason, when professionals do work in marginalized communities, it is important for research to be collaborative with community members' input to every step in the process, or with their input in the designing and implementation of professional services. But collaboration does not require professionals to subordinate their ideas and skills to those of community members. Collaboration is a relationship that respects the difference between professionals' (often indirect and technical) knowledge and community members' (often experiential and direct) knowledge and also supports efforts to join both forms of knowledge together under the umbrella of social justice work. This understanding rejects the view that members of oppressed communities can by themselves successfully challenge the structures of power and wealth that dominate them. It instead emphasizes the importance of bringing together different knowledge sets and different kinds of social networks to accomplish the difficult and complex challenges of attaining social justice today.

This volume consists of a series of articles exploring ways that professionals, armed with unique sets of knowledge and skills, and with a particular set of connections to governmental and corporate elites, can engage in social justice advocacy as participants and collaborators in community empowerment efforts. The contributors to this book are quite mindful of the warnings about professional social justice advocacy discussed above. Certainly, many professional advocacy organizations consist of advocates who take a stance that isolates them from the people for whom they advocate. And, as Piven and Cloward, Boyte, Warren, and others have shown with their "bottom-up" view of the problem, community organizers are rightfully leery of professionals out of a well-founded fear of co-optation and elitist domination that can undermine community empowerment efforts.[34]

The contributors to this volume, however, share the belief that professionals—academic researchers, teachers, lawyers, health care providers, social workers, and so forth—can and indeed should play important roles in social justice advocacy efforts. Indeed, effective social justice advocacy today often *requires* the participation of professionals, who can potentially deploy their skills and knowledge (what Bourdieu terms "cultural capital") and valuable contacts with institutional elites (Bourdieu's "social capital") in unique and constructive ways. The contributors to this volume share the view that social justice advocacy work by professionals can be most effective when it is done in the context of community empowerment. But the complex processes of the struggle for social justice requires the participation of people with specific professional expertise and connections to institutions of power, who can potentially play what Warren suggestively calls an "intermediary role" between community-based advocacy groups and the state and corporations.[35]

This intermediary role functions in two directions. Professionals can bring important resources to social justice movements. In their "top-down" role, professionals can use their "certified" knowledge and their social capital to legitimate marginalized people's problems and claims in the eyes of political and economic elites.[36] For example, when sociologists conduct research that substantiates minorities' claims of racial discrimination, this "validation," along with direct organizing work with elites, potentially helps build elite support for minorities' demands and helps foster cross-class, cross-race alliances and coalitions.

Professionals can also act as "bottom-up" liaisons to the state and corporations, conveying to political and economic elites the frames and demands of community-based social justice organizations. This function is particularly important, as it involves a specific form of intellectual activity that translates the ideologies of oppressed peoples (produced by a wide variety of organic intellectuals ranging from journalists to songwriters and performers) into forms that are recognized as valid by state and corporate actors. Thus lawyers who participate in social justice movements play an indispensable role translating the problems and demands of marginalized people into legal arguments and demands. By doing so, legal arguments and demands also become a component of the way oppressed people come to identify their problems and the solutions to them. Social scientists working with people demanding equity in access to public education can, with their research, develop ways of framing issues that help shape political elites' responses. And, perhaps most important, professionals can act as conveyers of power from below: acting as representatives of powerful social justice movements vastly multiplies the impact professionals can have in the realms of institutional power.

Community-based social justice work thus yields real benefits to professionals as well as to community needs. One of the main goals of this volume is to demonstrate that community-based social justice work can be a significant source of new insights that greatly enrich what is usually thought of as "professional" knowledge, as Pinderhughes demonstrates in his research on youth violence (chapter 5). Such collaborations can also magnify professionals' impact on policy debates and public consciousness, as Renée's and Pastor's chapters suggest. As well, as Loya shows, community-based social justice work has a transformative effect on the lives of both professionals and community-based advocates. Collaborative social justice work creates a remarkable synergetic relationship by linking community members and professionals together in a common effort to uphold the dignity and worth of marginalized people. For many professionals, such work also offers a valuable bridge out of a social world that is highly constricted by elitist class, race, and gender biases and offers new possibilities for the development of their intellectual and emotional self-understandings. This is especially compelling, of course, for professionals of color, who may find in community-based work a valuable respite from the racism that too often limits their careers and batters their self-esteem.[37] And, perhaps most important, community empowerment makes it possible for professionals who work for social justice to seriously undertake the process of democratizing their own disciplines and institutions (universities, law, health care, etc.).

We have now delineated traditional public professionalism from community-empowering social justice professionalism, and have also specified the intermediary role professionals can play in social justice work. We now turn to a recent history of social justice professionalism, to inquire into the processes that have made the questions of social justice and community empowerment increasingly important and pressing today.

Professionals and the Dialectic of Power in the Civil Rights Movement 1956–1975

Professional advocates had a very different relationship to grassroots social justice movement organizations in the era of mass insurgencies and welfare state politics—the 1950s until the mid-1970s—than they do now. An analysis of the relationships between professionals and social justice movements during that period is of value, both to better understand the forces that produced the "yawning gap" between professionals and grassroots social movements later and to glimpse a vision of the potential for such an organic relationship in the future.

While professionals have engaged in social justice work since the founding of the social sciences and helping professions, the relationships of professionals and social movements were most fully forged in the civil rights movement. The civil rights movement is correctly understood to be the most important social justice movement of the modern era. Its significance lay not only in its historic victory over Southern white power (the Jim Crow system) but also in its long-term impact on other efforts to advance social justice agendas in the United States.[38] The civil rights movement was initially rooted in a black community-based insurgency against the Jim Crow system.[39] But it was always more than this: it was also a multiracial, cross-class coalition in which different participants had very distinct agendas and interests.[40] The very first victory of the modern civil rights movement—the victory over segregated public transportation—was won not only by the adamant refusal of African Americans to ride segregated Montgomery buses but also by the ability of lawyers and political staffs to pressure the Interstate Commerce Commission to extend its power over local bus lines previously regulated by the states alone and to get federal courts to ratify this shift in power. Indeed, the strategic decision by black community activists to frame their grievances as a civil rights struggle was predicated on the predisposition of some (overwhelmingly white) political elites—primarily federal government officials—to expand protections for people of color against racial discrimination.[41] From the Montgomery bus boycott through the massive urban insurrections of 1964–1968 (the latter insurgencies aimed not at the Jim Crow system of the South but at the ghetto system of the North), some political elites saw the mobilization of power from below (i.e., autonomous from state power) as an opportunity to expand state (and their own) power from above. This was accomplished first through antidiscrimination rulings, statutes, and administrative procedures and later through active redistributive efforts such as the war on poverty; affirmative action in contracting, education, and employment; and school desegregation by racial assignment of students (busing).

The remarkable feature of this era was the synergistic relationship between insurgents' grassroots ideology and power and state ideology and power. Every advance in the capacity of communities of color to make effective demands was matched by the expansion of state power, and the expansion of state power created favorable conditions for a further extension of the demands for justice and the mobilization of grassroots power "from below." By 1966, however, the demands of the civil rights movement—for full employment, the end of the war in Vietnam, equity in educational opportunity, universal quality health care, access to decent housing for all, and so forth—had far outstripped the political capacity of movement participants to win the reforms they sought. However, confronted with urban insurrections and a losing war in Vietnam, political elites (including both Johnson and Nixon) continued to expand welfare state entitlements and civil rights programs for people of color, including affirmative action and the racial assignment of students to public schools.

The role of politicians and professionals in relation to the grassroots insurgencies against both the Jim Crow system and the ghetto system was, for the most part, a traditional, unidirectional, top-down relationship. There was often very little accountability of professionals or politicians to the grassroots movement: lawyers, politicians, health care providers, and academics developed their ideas, policies, and programs *in response to* protests but usually without collaborative relationships *with* grassroots activists. Thus, when lawyers first created housing clinics to advise poor tenants of their rights, they maintained their position as the source of expert knowledge. Similarly, when federal government officials expanded civil rights actions, they often did so without the direct participation of grassroots activists in their decisions.[42] Indeed, professional advocacy for social justice was often entrepreneurial in character, justifying the expansion of politicians' and professionals' power and authority. Of course, there have been notable exceptions, such as the Highlander Center, where professionals and community members have met to develop collaborative relationships since the 1930s.[43] However important they were for the development of the labor movement and the civil rights movement, these institutions were exceptions to the general trends of the welfare state era.

But for a brief time, as the civil rights movement gained maturity and power, professional involvement with social justice movements took on more of a collaborative relationship with grassroots groups, and some new forms of legal advocacy, health services, and education were briefly explored. At the peak of the urban insurrections against the ghetto system (1966–1968), a number of government programs and established private nonprofits were deftly usurped by grassroots activists. Quadagno explores the history of this era, showing how government programs, especially those created by the war on poverty initiatives, became important sites for community activists to gain access to both funding and influence that for a time could be and were used to benefit minority communities.[44] But community activists did not do so on their own: they were advised and represented by professionals at many crucial junctions.[45] Similarly, Jack Katz has detailed the ways legal aid lawyers developed new concepts of law and legal practices because of their organic ties to minority communities during this period.[46] This was also a period in which health professionals explored and advocated for new types of community-based health programs and educators collaborated with black, Puerto Rican, and Native American community-run schools.[47]

Despite these collaborative relationships of knowledge and power, as well as the initial success of activists' efforts to democratize institutions and of professionals to collaborate with poor people of color, efforts to develop collaborative community empowerment models remained very fragile and incomplete during this era. Quadagno shows, for example, the ways that vested political interests counterattacked when community empowerment efforts were initiated, and wrested control of local school boards and community block grants away from community activists. Katz chronicles the attacks on the Legal Aid Society, which defunded most of its community-based legal clinics by the mid-1970s. The vision and practice of community-based professional advocacy was short-lived and fragile, and the practice of this collaborative relationship was achieved for only a few short years during the maximum mobilization of grassroots power (1966–1970). Despite these weaknesses, the vision of such work is one of the important legacies of the era of mass protest in the late 1960s and early 1970s.

The social movements of that era had other important long-term impacts on many professions. Participation in social movements convinced hundreds of thousands of movement participants to seek professional degrees. The civil rights and antiwar movements had disproportionately attracted college students from selective institutions of higher education who were already on professional career tracks.[48] While their motivation and capacity were considerably different from that of the Southern black community activists who formed the backbone of the civil rights movement, college students (who were likely to be white) were typically forever changed by their experiences in that movement.[49] As Fendrich has shown with his thirty-year longitudinal study of movement participants, young white participants in the civil rights movement made significantly different choices in careers, spouses, and friends than whites that did not participate in the movement.[50] Movement experience did not only transform elite college students. Some activists whose parents were sharecroppers, migrant workers, or blue-collar workers also began to appreciate the value of professional credentials as a form of resource mobilization by and for social movements and were given important cultural and social capital "bridges" into credentialing institutions through their elite contacts in social justice movements.[51] These experiences, coupled with the expansion of public institutions of higher education, led to a significant increase in the percentage of young African Americans and Latinos to become first-generation college graduates during the 1970s.[52]

The massive uprisings of the late 1960s and early 1970s were quite brief in duration: by the middle of the decade, they were mostly gone. But the extraordinary energy of that time propelled a generation of young people influenced by these movements into universities, government jobs, and nonprofit organizations. It is to their experiences since then that we now turn.

The Crisis of Social Justice Advocacy in the Global Era

The profound gap between young professionals with social justice agendas and grassroots "publics" was apparent even in the 1970s. Michael Burawoy, one of the leading figures in radical American sociology since the 1970s, describes it this way:

> Revisiting "radical sociology" of the 1970s one cannot but be struck by its unrepentant academic character, both in its analytical style and its substantive remoteness. It mirrored the world it sought to conquer. For all of its radicalism its immediate object was the transformation of sociology not of society. Like those Young Hegelians of whom Marx and Engels spoke so contemptuously we were fighting phrases with phrases, making revolutions with words. Our theoretical obsessions came not from the lived experiences or common sense of subaltern classes, but from the contradictions and anomalies of our research programs. The audiences for our reinventions of Marxism, and our earnest diatribes against bourgeois sociology were not agents of history—workers, peasants, minorities—but a narrow body of intellectuals, largely cut off from the world they claimed to represent.[53]

Burawoy's account for one academic discipline also holds true for radical law, radical public health, and radical education during that era. Social justice activists who had entered professional schools during the 1970s found themselves gradually cut off from the social movements in which they had participated and from minority communities that had formed the base of these movements. Social justice advocates entering the professions increasingly defined their work by criteria acceptable within the professions.

There are many factors that led radical professionals to turn inward to their own professions and away from community-based movements. The most important reason was the ebb in mass social justice movements after the mid-1970s.[54] As we have seen, the movements had both engendered and legitimized new ways of thinking within professions. Their decline placed social justice advocates in a much weaker position to pursue an agenda set by these movements within their professions. A second factor was the curtailment of the welfare state, which first was manifested as "fiscal crises" that bankrupted a number of major urban governments in the mid-1970s.[55] The retraction of government social justice programs—including new limitations on desegregation of public schools, jobs, public health, and housing—deprived social justice professionals of access to resources, including public sector jobs in universities, schools, hospitals, and other government agencies. A third factor undermining social justice professionals' connection to marginalized communities was that the vast majority of them were young newcomers to their professions who lacked legitimacy and claims to institutional resources within their professions. Thus, for young radical professionals, the bottom line was that they needed to either conform to professional elites' expectations to get jobs and grants, or, as happened in American sociology, history, and economics in the 1970s, they could undertake the protracted struggle described by Burawoy to dethrone the old guard. But, in either case, young radicals had to pay their dues to get their professional credentials and to secure positions within their professions, tasks that required them to turn inward to their own professions. Of course, not all radical professionals did this: an untold story of the 1970s and 1980s is that of thousands of young, aspiring academics, lawyers, and health professionals who dropped out of graduate programs or were denied jobs in their fields because of their commitment to social justice. As well, thousands of other professionals accepted marginal (i.e., low-paying, low-status) positions in their fields precisely so that they could continue to participate in social justice movements.[56]

Even in the late 1970s and early 1980s, however, social justice movements (such as the antiapartheid, Central America solidarity, gay liberation, and pro-choice movements) were powerful enough to confer some legitimacy and influence to some professionals, at least those who articulated the movements' agendas in ways that did not undermine their professions' commitment to scholarship. As well, the application of the civil rights model to a variety of new social justice issues—women's rights, gay and lesbian rights, environmental protection, and so forth—maintained some of the momentum of the 1960s flow well into the 1980s.[57]

The gap between marginal communities' efforts to achieve social justice and professionals advocating for social justice issues became qualitatively greater in the 1980s and 1990s. In those decades, efforts to dismantle the welfare state increased in pace and power, not only in the United States but also in Europe and Japan. Regulatory regimes were vilified for placing barriers in the way of "free" market activities. Redistributive policies were assaulted for undermining productivity by allegedly overly taxed corporations and wealthy individuals. In place of the welfare state, a new ideology envisioning a "private accumulation" state was articulated, one in which the primary responsibility of government is to foster the private accumulation of wealth and to protect wealth from "bad people," often labeled criminals and terrorists.[58]

These developments are political manifestations of the current trends of globalization.[59] In the last two decades, new technologies have enabled capital to flow more rapidly around the world, giving transnational investors greater leverage over governments with the credible threat that if governments don't deregulate businesses and lower taxes on them, investment would just flow elsewhere.[60] The new technologies have also engendered a new division of labor, with growing wage inequality between knowledge-based and labor service work. In these ways, the current phase of globalization is marked by rapidly growing inequality and the erosion of government's ability to intervene in the name of social justice or social stability.

These developments have placed advocates for social justice on the defensive. Progressive lawyers, for example, find themselves expending more energy keeping cases away from the U.S. Supreme Court than in seeking justice from it. Worse still, the "fear of falling" that grips much of the middle class, coupled with the erosion of governmental support for community-based initiatives, and the increasing geographical mobility of people seeking work, are rapidly eroding the social ties that create communities and give people a context in which to publicly articulate their own interests.[61] Right-wing politicians eagerly channel the fear that potential loss of middle-class respectability and stability engenders into a fear of criminals, immigrants, and terrorists. The right-wing formula has galvanized massive support, as tens of millions of frightened Americans have rejected an expansive sense of their civic world and have replaced it with a small worldview, narrowly bounded by race and class.[62]

The retraction of state-supported services and the growing inequality of income and wealth have had a disproportionate impact on racial and ethnic minority communities.[63] As government programs are cut, those with the most private assets—who are disproportionately whites—are most likely to be able to purchase housing, education, and health care, while those with little assets—mostly people of color—are more likely to be left with no safety net. The staggering tale exposed by Hurricane Katrina of long-term criminal neglect and the callous governmental disregard of the plight of New Orleans's black poor is a horrific example of the extent of societal disinterest in the plight of poor people of color today.[64] To a less extreme extent than the Lower 9th Ward, many inner city ghettoes and barrios have been stripped of public support for quality education, housing, and jobs.[65] But, even in such horrendous conditions, the varied histories of ethnic solidarity, combined with ongoing resistance to racism, continually reproduce formal and informal ties among people of color.[66]

All of these developments have negatively impacted professional advocates for social justice, particularly those who work for government agencies or the "memberless" nonprofit organizations advocating for (silenced) people created in the 1970s and 1980s. These advocates relied heavily on public sector and foundation support for their work and, during the 1990s and after, have found the flow of money and public sector jobs drastically curtailed. Political elites and funders who control those resources now restrict the range of policy options considered acceptable, further limiting the scope of professionals' social justice advocacy. During the 1990s, professional advocates found themselves in an increasingly untenable situation, desperately defending the victories of the late 1960s and early 1970s (and losing ground rapidly) but by and large unable to articulate new visions of social justice or tactics for achieving it. Confronted by growing inequality, increasingly potent attacks on the welfare state model, and an aggressively self-confident and well-organized right-wing movement able to exploit the new conditions, professional advocates for social justice have found themselves in a full-blown crisis, as their claims that they are able to represent the interests of oppressed peoples have become increasingly implausible.

The Possibilities for Social Justice Advocacy in the Global Era

What, given this difficult history, can professional advocates for social justice do to make themselves more effective? Here, I suggest a deceptively simple answer: *they must change their relationship to power.*

An inquiry into the possibilities for a future resurgence of social justice advocacy requires first a deeper look at the dynamics of globalization itself. While globalization has empowered capital and weakened the state in new ways discussed above, it is also creating new possibilities for those adversely affected by growing inequalities of opportunity. There are two important developments that give rise to at least cautious optimism for the future of social justice. One is that globalization is rapidly transforming where marginalized people live. Second, globalization is creating new conditions that demand a revitalized role for nation-states in order to maintain social stability.

Globalization has ushered in the most rapid geographical mobility of humanity in all of history.[67] This mass migration is remarkable not only in its quantity but also its direction. People from all over the world are now moving in large numbers into the urban centers of the nations that are the headquarters of transnational corporations (TNCs), that is, the United States and Europe.[68] The new migration is also distinctive in that it is bimodal, bringing to the "global cities" of the North a mix of a small number of high-skilled knowledge service workers and a large mass of low-skilled manufacturing and labor service workers. The net effect of the new migration has been to rapidly swell the ranks of people who are designated as racial minorities in all of the developed countries. In the United States, where some 35 percent of all new immigrants come from Mexico and 70 percent from Latin America and Asia, the large growth in the Latino and Asian populations has already had an impact on American politics and culture. The new immigration, says Sassen, has already produced large and increasingly marginalized shadow populations within the global cities of the United States and Europe. These "subter-ranean" people, Sassen predicts, will not stay in the shadows indefinitely.[69] As inequality becomes more extreme, and as repressive measures against people of color increase, the explosion of immigrant populations, created by the im-personal forces of globalization, may well make ethnic communities' efforts to resist repression into a vital force in American urban and national politics in the years to come.[70] While Putnam and Skocpol are correct in their estima-tion of the weakening of civic society for the white middle class, the growth of immigrant ethnic communities may well be an important countertrend. As the numbers and intensity of the marginalization of immigrants and nonim-migrant people of color increase, it may well be that the intensity of the so-cial networks that create ethnic communities will increase as well. If so, eth-nic communities may become increasingly important counters to the loss of state and civil society sketched out above.

The growing numbers and potential organization of "ethnicized" peoples are found in concert with another social trend: the destabilization of the mid-dle-class social order. The middle-class order is largely the product of the wel-fare state policies of the post–World War II era.[71] The assault on living wages and benefits (both private and public), as well as the rising cost of housing, health care, and education, has left much of the U.S. workforce with a pre-carious relationship to the idea of the middle class. Declining standards of living and the rising private cost of housing, education, and health care are politically destabilizing the social order that for the last sixty years has rested on the expansion of the middle class. The rise of gated communities, Chris-tian fundamentalism, American xenophobia, and white racism bear bleak testimony to the loss of hope of much of the middle class today.

But the destabilization of the middle-class social order also contains a ray of hope. As Polanyi has shown, the precondition to market success is social stability.[72] Globalization today is developing primarily through the expansion of global markets. While cultural and political/legal globalizations are also emerging, they are dominated by the neoliberal ideology of "free trade." *The problem for transnational corporations, as well as for everyone else, is that market globalization—marked by the eradication of national arrangements—is undermin-ing social orders, and therefore social stability, everywhere.* Growing inequality, and assaults on the capacities of states to regulate markets, cannot do any-thing but produce social instability. And, as Polanyi warns, market relation-ships (and, especially, profit-making) cannot succeed in the absence of polit-ical and civic social stability.

The destruction of the American middle-class social order, as well as the architecture for social stability in all other nations and in the international arrangements painstakingly constructed throughout the twentieth century, cannot be in the long-term interests of TNCs. Sooner or later—and I believe sooner—global capital will have to enter into negotiations with those who are currently being marginalized or cut out entirely from the benefits of globalization.[73] In the absence of significant global political arrangements, nation-states, the only institutions capable of organizing social stability, will continue to occupy center stage in these negotiations.[74] But so might well-organized nongovernmental groups capable of exerting political pressure on nation-states. In a period of social destabilization, the potential impact of ethnic community-based advocates for social justice might become far greater than it is today.

This analysis suggests that the role of professional advocates for social justice may be far brighter in the future than in the current period. If the demand for measures aimed at social stabilization—including both regulating markets and developing redistributive social programs—becomes increasingly pressing, professionals will be called upon to use their expertise to design and implement effective social policy. In particular, if people currently excluded from the benefits of globalization develop significant political power, then professional advocates for social justice may find themselves in a new position vis-à-vis both social movements and the state: the role of intermediary may become a specialized and valuable component of the search for social order in the future.

But a caveat is immediately required: professionals' expertise will be relevant to the future debates over social policy only to the extent that their ideas are transformed into political power. Archon Fung and Erik Olin Wright have already discerned this point; they challenge intellectuals to engage in the revitalization of participatory democracy, but at the same time they recognize the necessity of the deployment of countervailing power to enable democratic innovations.[75] It is precisely this point that requires professional advocates for social justice to readjust their roles in the present period. For far too long, professional advocates have clung to the dreams of the past, fighting desperate defensive battles to save vestiges of the programs and policies created during the period of the expansion of the welfare state. As we have already seen, this stance has come at a cost, as professional advocates have become increasingly isolated politically and intellectually from the communities they claim to represent. The potential new openings for social justice to again become politically relevant requires that advocates turn their attention to a new task: the development of new relationships to the communities that may in the future have an important say in whatever new social policies are considered to restabilize society.

The realignment of professional advocacy toward collaborative relationships with advocates for marginalized communities is an enormous undertaking and is far more significant than just a shift in the recipients of professional services. Here I will briefly outline some of the challenges, all discussed in later chapters of this book:

1. The production of knowledge/cultural capital: Professional advocates whose practices are bound to the state or private sector take as the starting point for research the existing parameters of policy options that are considered acceptable in those settings. Professional advocates whose practices are bound to marginalized communities have a far different agenda, one that is driven by community demands for social justice, and not what is considered "realistic" by insiders. As a result, this new orientation challenges and broadens conceptualizations of social problems and solutions to them, greatly deepening and expanding the potential sources of professional knowledge. As contributors to this volume show, collaboration between advocates and professionals actively shapes the research topics, research methods, ability to collect relevant data, products of research, and methods of their dissemination.

2. The development of social capital: Professional advocates whose practices are bound to the state or the private sector recognize the importance of social capital and work assiduously to develop ties to other insiders: legislative and regulatory staffs, foundations, media outlets, and so forth. Professional advocates whose practices are bound to marginalized communities are faced with a far more complex task: they must simultaneously develop all of these institutional ties, as well as develop their ties to the community in which their work is rooted. The development of social networks within the community is itself a major undertaking, as Mark Warren describes.[76] And, most significantly, given the choice of developing "insider" connections with elites or building ties in the community, advocates must choose the latter over the former, for it is the ties to the community that ultimately give advocates the power that will make their collaborative agenda relevant.

3. The contradictions of community-based professional advocacy: Professional community-based advocacy is a doubly marginalizing process. As professional advocates redefine their expertise and their social capital in terms set by marginal communities, they are virtually certain to be penalized by traditional professional insiders. Advocates who are bound to marginal communities typically have their ideas dismissed as "biased" and have a far more difficult time getting support for their research. Ad-

vocacy work is dismissed as merely "applied" activity, while the development of knowledge by and for political elites is upheld as "pure" research. In academic settings, community-based professional advocacy is seldom rewarded in terms of publication, hiring, promotion, and tenure decisions. Indeed, many academic advocates report that their work remains invisible within their professions.[77] By focusing on the development of community-based social networks, professional advocates are also marginalized from insider networks. Professional advocates are not only marginalized within their professions—they are also marginal to communities with whom they ally. Professional knowledge and social networks, even those developed by and for marginal communities, are distinct from other forms of knowledge and networks. Indeed, the tasks of community-based social justice advocacy place professionals in the position of being permanent outsiders. But this is how it should be: The task of social justice advocacy requires professionals to act as intermediaries, translating demands for social justice into forms of knowledge and policies that are acceptable within the realm of state power, and translating community-based power into forms of power that can make these ideas and policies into real reforms. In this sense, professional advocates are neither insiders nor outsiders, but are both simultaneously.

4. Professional advocates as "intermediaries": Despite these problems, the newfound interest in public professionalism, primarily by traditional professionals, opens up new possibilities for professional advocates working collaboratively with organizers of marginalized and oppressed communities. It is possible, in the space now opening up for public intellectuals, that those professionals linked to social justice movements will demonstrate that their access to community-based power and the frames of reference of marginalized people make them far more effective than traditional public intellectuals limited to critiquing existing social arrangements. But community-based professionals will succeed in making inroads in their professions and with political elites only if they engage in activities deemed legitimate within their professions. For academic professionals, for example, social justice advocacy must entail simultaneously participation in community-based activities and participation in the types of reflexive activities (research, publishing in peer review journals) of their professions. It is incumbent on social justice professionals to demonstrate the link between activism and knowledge, not to appease traditional professionals and political elites but because professionals' specialized knowledge and potential elite influence is of value to community-based advocacy efforts.

Conclusion: Public Professionalism
and Advocacy for Social Justice

This chapter outlines a series of tasks for those committed to nurturing community-based public professionalism. It suggests that efforts to transform civic consciousness must take into account the stratification of society, both to understand the emerging opportunities for social justice and to accurately grasp the identities of the potential agents of change. It further suggests that those who seek to engage with the most marginal and oppressed communities face a different set of challenges and possibilities for public professionalism than do those who work in the context of elite politics. The most important conclusion of this analysis is that collaborative public professionalism rooted in marginal and oppressed communities is potentially transformative of civic consciousness in that it provides new types of linkages to expertise and power and is simultaneously transformative of professionalism, as it challenges and expands conceptions of knowledge and professional practice.

The analysis above further suggests that community-based social justice advocacy should be expected to become increasingly important in both these dimensions as the possibilities for "insider" social justice advocacy diminish and as the demands for social justice by marginalized communities increase in salience. As professionals take the radical step of turning away from the "top down world of memberless organizations" and experience the excitement and exigencies of working from the "bottom up," it is important to remember the "Polanyi problem": the screw will turn, and the demands for social justice from those currently bearing the brunt of the social crisis of globalization will become more significant as societies—America included—experience growing destabilization. It is fascinating to think of the period soon to come, when advocates for social justice will be able to challenge old ideas and the old social order these ideas defend in a way that has not been seen since the 1960s and 1930s. Professional advocates positioned as intermediaries between marginalized communities and the state may well find the coming period as immensely rewarding as this time has been so hard.

Notes

1. Sidney Tarrow, *Power in Movement* (London: Cambridge University Press, 1998); Doug McAdam, *Political Processes and the Development of Black Insurgency, 1930–1970* (Chicago: University of Chicago Press, 1982).

2. Martin Luther King Jr., "Letter from Birmingham Jail," in *Why We Can't Wait* (New York: Harper and Row, 1964).

3. Joel Krieger, *Reagan, Thatcher, and the Politics of Decline* (Cambridge: Polity Press, 1986).

4. No one understood this better, or did it better, than Lyndon Baines Johnson. See Robert Caro, *The Years of Lyndon Johnson: Master of the Senate* (New York: Alfred A. Knopf, 2002).

5. Jill Quadagno, "Creating a Capital Investment Welfare State: The New American Exceptionalism," presidential address to the American Sociological Association 1998, *American Sociological Review* 64 (February 1999): 1–11.

6. Harold R. Karbo, *Social Stratification and Inequality* (New York: McGraw Hill, 2000), esp. 24.

7. Richard Ericson and Aaron Doyle, "Globalization and the Policing of Protest: The Case of APEC 1997," *British Journal of Sociology* 50, no. 4 (December 1999): 589–608.

8. Andrew L. Barlow, *Between Fear and Hope: Globalization and Race in the United States* (Lanham, MD: Rowman & Littlefield, 2003).

9. Theda Skocpol, *Diminished Democracy: From Membership to Management in American Civic Life* (Norman: University of Oklahoma Press, 2003), 139–40.

10. This gap has been on full display in the historic upsurge of the immigrant rights movement that began in February 2006. While advocacy organizations provided some scaffolding for demonstrations, this movement is to a great extent a spontaneous expression of Latinos' frustration with their isolation from political influence at a time of their greatly growing numbers in American society.

11. Michael Burawoy, "Public Sociologies: Contradictions, Dilemmas and Possibilities" and response articles in *Social Problems* 82, 4 (June 2004).

12. The American Sociological Association Task Force on the Institutionalization of Public Sociology website is pubsoc.wisc.edu/. The American Historical Association website is www.historians.org/governance/tfph/. The public anthropologist website is www.publicanthropology.org/.

13. One such effort is the Equal Justice Society, www.equaljusticesociety.org/.

14. One example includes the efforts of social scientists, health professionals, and lawyers to defeat Proposition 54 in California in 2003. See Andrew Barlow and Troy Duster, "Researchers Challenge California Initiative to Ban Racial Data," *American Sociological Association Footnotes* (July/August 2003): 3.

15. Outstanding examples of social science briefs can be found in the U.S. Supreme Court case of *Meredith vs. Jefferson County* (05-915). All of the amicus curiae briefs can be found at the NAACP Legal Defense Fund website.

16. One model is the Media Research and Action Project, developed by William Gamson and Charlene Ryan. The institute, based at Boston College, trains community advocacy groups in media work.

17. Chris Mooney, *The Republican War on Science* (New York: Basic Books, 2005).

18. Lewis Mumford, *The Culture of Cities* (New York: Harcourt, Brace, 1996); Robert Bellah, *The Broken Covenant: American Civil Religion in a Time of Trial* (Chicago: University of Chicago Press, 1992).

19. Michael Burawoy, "For a Sociological Marxism: The Complementary Convergence of Antonio Gramsci and Karl Polanyi," *Politics & Society* 31, no. 2 (June 2003): 193–261.

20. Burawoy, "Public Sociologies."

21. Paul Osterman, *Gathering Power: The Future of Progressive Politics in America* (Boston: Beacon Press, 2002), 82–83.

22. Aldon Morris has explored the role of the black church in the civil rights movement in *The Origins of the Civil Rights Movement: Black Communities Organizing for Change* (New York: Free Press, 1984). For a useful discussion of grassroots social movements, see Mark Warren, *Dry Bones Rattling: Community Building to Revitalize American Democracy* (Princeton, NJ: Princeton University Press, 2001).

23. Melvin L. Oliver, "The Urban Black Community as Network: Towards a Social Network Perspective," *Sociological Quarterly* 29, no. 4 (Winter 1988): 623–45.

24. Duncan Kennedy, "Legal Education as Training for Hierarchy," in *The Politics of Law*, ed. David Kairys (New York: Pantheon Books, 1982), 45.

25. William L. Felsteiner, Richard Abel, and Austin Sarat, "The Emergence and Transformation of Disputes: Naming, Blaming and Claiming," *Law and Society Review* 9, no. 3–4 (1980–1981): 631–95.

26. Eric Hobsbawm, *The Age of Extremes* (London: Michael Joseph, 1994), 428.

27. Frank Parkin, *Marxism and Class Theory: A Bourgeois Critique* (London: Tavistock, 1979).

28. On cultures of resistance, see Henry Giroux, *Schooling and the Struggle for Public Life* (Boulder, CO: Paradigm Publishers, 2005). On self-help networks, see Carol Stack, *All Our Kin: Strategies for Survival in a Black Community* (New York: Basic Books, 1997).

29. Ruth Milkman, *Organizing Immigrants: The Challenge for Unions in Contemporary California* (Ithaca, NY: Cornell University Press, 2000). See also Pierrette Hondagneu-Sotelo, *Domestica: Immigrant Workers Cleaning and Caring in the Shadows of Affluence* (Berkeley: University of California Press, 2001).

30. See Marlon Riggs's documentary film, *Tongues Untied*; Martin Manalansan, *Global Divas: Gay Men in the Diaspora* (Durham, NC: Duke University Press, 2003).

31. Harry C. Boyte, *Everyday Politics: Reconnecting Citizens and Public Life* (Philadelphia: University of Pennsylvania Press, 2004), xii.

32. Frances Fox Piven and Richard Cloward, *Regulating the Poor* (London: Tavistock, 1972), 175–76.

33. This formulation is a significant point of departure from many of the fine scholars who are engaging in community-based research (CBR). See Randy Stoeker, *Community-Based Research* (Sage Publications, 2004).

34. Saul Alinsky once put this bias bluntly: "[T]he word 'academic' is a synonym for irrelevant." Saul Alinsky, *Reveille for Radicals* (New York: Vintage Books, 1969 [1946]), ix.

35. Warren, *Dry Bones*, chap. 1.

36. Magalli Sarfatti Larson, *The Rise of the Professionals* (Berkeley: University of California Press, 1977).

37. Roslyn Arlin Mickelson, Samuel Stephen, and Melvin L. Oliver, "Breaking Through the Barriers: African American Job Candidates and the Academic Hiring Process," in *Beyond Silenced Voices: Class, Race and Gender in United States Schools*, ed. Lois Weiss and Michelle Fine (Albany: State University of New York Press, 1993), 9–24.

38. Tarrow, *Power in Movement*; McAdam, *Political Processes*.

39. Morris, *Origins of the Civil Rights Movement*.

40. Jack M. Bloom, *Class, Race and the Civil Rights Movement* (Bloomington: Indiana University Press, 1987).

41. Max Weber defines *civil rights* as "government claims to protect behavior from discrimination," in *Economy and Society*, ed. Guenther Roth and Claus Wittich (Berkeley: University of California Press, 1978).

42. Juan Williams, *Thurgood Marshall: American Revolutionary* (New York: Times Books, 1998).

43. On the Highlander Center, see Dale Jacobs, ed., *The Myles Horton Reader: Education for Social Change* (Knoxville: University of Tennessee Press, 2003).

44. Jill Quadagno, *The Color of Welfare: How Racism Undermined the War on Poverty* (New York: Oxford University Press, 1994).

45. See the discussion of lawyers and judges in the development of community-based grassroots social justice organizations in Dan Georgakis and Marvin Surkin, *Detroit: I Do Mind Dying* (Boston: South End Press, 2003 [1978]).

46. Jack Katz, *Poor People's Lawyers in Transition* (New Brunswick, NJ: Rutgers University Press, 1982).

47. On community-controlled schools during the Black Power movement, see Wendell Pritchett, *Brownsville, Brooklyn: Blacks, Jews and the Changing Face of the Ghetto* (Chicago: University of Chicago Press, 2002).

48. Everett Carll Ladd Jr. and Seymour Martin Lipset, *Professors, Unions, and American Higher Education* (Washington, DC: American Enterprise Institute for Public Policy Research, 1973).

49. Andrew L. Barlow, "The Student Movements of the 1960s and the Politics of Race," *The Journal of Ethnic Studies* 19 (Fall 1991): 3–22.

50. James Fendrich, *Ideal Citizens: The Legacy of the Civil Rights Movement* (Albany: State University of New York Press, 1993).

51. Carlos Muñoz Jr., *Youth Identity and Power: The Sixties Chicano Movement* (London: Verso Press, 1989).

52. David Karen reports a tripling of the percentage of black eighteen- to twenty-four-year-olds enrolled in college between 1960 (7 percent) and 1975 (22.6 percent). The ratio of black to white eighteen- to twenty-four-year-olds in college also rose from 32 percent in 1960 to 85 percent in 1975. David Karen, "The Politics of Class, Race, and Gender: Access to Higher Education in the United States 1960–1986," *American Journal of Education* 99, 2 (February 1991): 208–37. See Muñoz, *Youth Identity*, for a description of first-generation Chicano students in this period.

53. Michael Burawoy, "The Critical Turn to Public Sociology," in *Enriching the Sociological Imagination: How Radical Sociology Enriched the Discipline*, ed. Rhonda F. Levine (Leiden: Brill, 2004), 309.

54. For an account of the ebb of the civil rights movement, see Barlow, *Between Fear and Hope*, chaps. 6–7. The antiwar movement entered a period of crisis after the withdrawal of American troops from Vietnam began in 1973, and certainly after the Vietnamese victory in 1975.

55. James O'Connor, *The Fiscal Crisis of the State*, 2nd ed. (New Brunswick, NJ: Transaction, 2002).

56. At this point, I would like to point out that this author is tenured in the California community college system, as well as being a visiting professor at the University of California at Berkeley. My decision to base my academic career in the community colleges was precisely made to afford me greater space to engage in social justice activism than the highly proscribed tenure process a research university allows. On the other hand, my ability to bridge between the community colleges and Berkeley was in part based on my decision, in the 1970s, to retreat from activism in order to pursue a PhD from Harvard University, as well as regularly publishing in academic journals. Without this degree and publications, and the cultural and social capital that came with them, I would not have been able to develop such a two-track career, which has been beneficial for both my activism and my academic work.

57. Tarrow, *Power in Movement*, refers to cycles of protest to explain this phenomenon.

58. Goran Therborn, *The Western European Welfare State and Its Hostile World* (Madrid: Centro de Estudios Avanzados en Ciencias Sociales, Instituto Juan March de Estudios e Investigaciones, 1997).

59. For an overview, see Barlow, *Between Fear and Hope*, chap. 3.

60. Saskia Sassen, *Globalization and Its Discontents* (New York: New Press, 1998).

61. Robert Putnam, *Bowling Alone: The Collapse and Revival of American Community* (New York: Simon & Schuster, 2000).

62. Lee Cokorenos, *The Assault on Diversity* (Lanham, MD: Rowman & Littlefield, 2003).

63. Barlow, *Between Fear and Hope*.

64. Wealth inequality has steadily worsened, especially in the past decade. Rakesh Kochhar, *The Wealth of Hispanic Households: 1996–2002* (Washington, DC: Pew Hispanic Center, 2004).

65. William Julius Wilson, *When Work Disappears* (New York: Random House, 1997).

66. Yen Le Espiritu, "Theories of Ethnicity," in *The Social Construction of Race and Ethnicity in the United States*, 2nd ed., ed. Joan Ferrante and Prince Browne Jr. (Upper Saddle River, NJ: Prentice Hall, 2001), 257–63.

67. Nigel Harris, *The New Untouchables* (New York: St. Martin's Press, 1995).

68. Sassen, *Globalization*.

69. Saskia Sassen, *Guests and Aliens* (New York: New Press, 1999).

70. The immigrant communities of France have certainly shown the potential for such insurgencies, as have the massive mobilizations in the United States against HR4437 in February–May 2006.

71. Barlow, *Between Fear and Hope*, chap. 2.

72. Karl Polanyi, *The Great Transformation: The Political and Economic Origins of Our Time* (Boston: Beacon Press, 2001 [1945]), also Burawoy, "Sociological Marxism"; Peter Evans, "Counter-hegemonic Globalization: Transnational Social Movements in the Contemporary Global Political Economy," in *The Handbook of Political Sociology*, eds. Thomas Janoski, Alexander M. Hicks, and Mildred Schwartz (New York: Cambridge University Press, 2005).

73. In some ways, this is already happening in Latin America, especially in Brazil, Venezuela, and Bolivia.

74. The continuing centrality of nation-states in the global era has been well analyzed by Malcolm Waters, *Globalization* (London: Routledge, 2001), chap. 5.

75. Archon Fong and Erik Olin Wright, eds., *Deepening Democracy* (London: Verso Press, 2003).

76. Warren, *Dry Bones*.

77. This is a key finding of the Report to the American Sociological Association by the Task Force for the Institutionalization of Public Sociology.

~

CHAPTER TWO

Creating a New World: Transformative Lawyering for Social Change

Anamaria Loya

I am the executive director of La Raza Centro Legal—a nonprofit social justice center located in San Francisco. La Raza Centro Legal is not a typical legal aid organization in that we not only address people's legal concerns and we do not simply provide free legal representation. We do those things, but we also focus on much more. We seek to be transformative in our work and to empower individuals and communities.

What do I mean by this? I mean much more than community mobilizing, organizing, or educating. I mean that we seek to create long-term complete transformation in people's lives. Our work is not only change-oriented; we are not just trying to change something that already exists. We are also being creative—building or creating something new. For example, we seek to create a new reality in which an undocumented immigrant woman who earns her income as a domestic worker is not just a needy client with a wage claim or an immigration problem. She is not powerless. In our work, she may become the head of a women's collective of domestic workers determining their own minimum wage, engaging in job development, educating employers about safe and green housecleaning products, and creating alliances and movement among domestic workers and other low-wage workers to create local and statewide policies that protect and uphold their rights in the workplace. In other words, she is a very powerful, influential individual who can impact our community.

Being creative and not just reactive is extremely difficult. We often fail. The forces that devalue and exploit undocumented immigrants, for example, can seem insurmountably powerful. There are times when our own actions— such as making a decision for an immigrant client instead of making it *with* the client—fail to re-create a world where immigrants are powerfully involved in their own destiny.

While there may be models of transformative empowerment lawyering elsewhere, in my own personal experience I have not been exposed to this orientation outside of La Raza Centro Legal. From my own personal experience, I know that we are not taught in law school to engage in empowerment work or movement building. Often this work feels uncertain, new, as if every day we are learning and exploring new ground. Yet, the type of work we engage in is exactly what I had once very naively assumed all lawyers did.

When I was growing up, my parents were both educators and we lived in the Coachella Valley in Southern California. At that time, in the late 1960s and 1970s, agriculture was a significant industry in the area. There were many farmworker families in the community in which I grew up. My parents both became very involved in social justice work. They organized for the farmworkers, were committed to the educational advancement of people of color and disenfranchised people, especially Chicano/Latinos, published a Chicano newspaper called *Ideal*, picketed, protested, sued, educated, and were overall very politically active. My parents' activism has had a powerful impact on me and my life, has given me tremendous blessings, and has also created huge challenges for our family. These early experiences in my life, I believe, greatly influence why I was drawn to work at La Raza Centro Legal and why I value the type of transformative work that we engage in.

The activism of my parents was met with repression. My dad was arrested, convicted, and served time for organizing a peaceful demonstration in which the crowd clapped in unison to drown out a politician who was speaking. Later, based on the First Amendment, the California Supreme Court overturned his conviction, but only after he served sixty-two days in jail just after my younger sister was born. When I was five years old I went with my dad to the hospital to visit my mom and my new baby sister. The very next day, my dad was gone, my mom and great-grandmother were in tears, and I was confused and scared. I didn't link the upset in our family at that time to the political activism of my parents. I just remember feeling fear, missing my dad, and knowing that something was wrong. I also remember later feeling pride and relief when he was able to come back home. At the time, I was not aware of the role the law and lawyers played in that family drama. I just knew that my dad was back and things were finally okay. However, as years passed, I began to form a definite opinion of lawyers and the law.

My dad struggled with being constantly attacked publicly in the press and at school among his colleagues. He was regularly passed up for promotion despite often being the most qualified, trained, educated, and licensed candidate for an opening. He was directly told that if he would give up his "rabble-rousing" on behalf of the Mexicans, he would be able to be promoted. Instead of giving up that "rabble-rousing" he sued the school district. That lawsuit lasted eight years and never resulted in a court ruling in my dad's favor. However, immediately after filing the lawsuit, he began to see career advancement. The lawyer who represented my dad in that lawsuit was a Chicano lawyer from Napa, California, named Louis Flores. He was my first role model for a lawyer. I was in awe of him. I was convinced that all lawyers were like Louis Flores—they fought for the underdog, were fiercely committed to social justice, and knew a lot about good-quality wine.

These early experiences planted in me a strong commitment to fight for social justice. My dad's style was to fight for what was right, to "stick it" to the "bad guys," and even to mock or humiliate the "enemy." The repression we experienced was so real and palpable that this probably lent to my dad's style of fighting for social justice. We did not always feel safe in our community. I remember once a local grower tried to run over my dad and me on a public street. The IRS audited our family several years in a row. We often received threatening and frightening anonymous telephone calls. My father struggled with alcoholism during these years. My mom, dad, and great-grandmother struggled with trying to raise a secure and healthy family amidst the overwhelming pressures and turmoil.

Yet we were also tremendously blessed. I always remember feeling significant and important. Every week, there were people coming to our house seeking help from my family. Wherever we went in town, people knew who we were. I was an extremely shy child, and when we had visitors, my favorite thing to do was to sit quietly, almost invisible, and listen to the grownups talk. I would hear a farmworker and his wife explain to my mom and dad their plight, how they were treated unfairly, and how they needed help. I would hear my dad respond with authority and assurance. He would identify how the problem would be resolved and what we would all do to help them. I felt overwhelming pride in those moments, and those moments were regular occurrences.

As a child, I carried picket signs in front of Safeway with my mom. I rolled up *Ideal* newspapers and threw them at people's homes, and left stacks at the local Circle K store. I remember playing the piano for organizers and hearing them say, "That's good *mija*. Now, can you play a *ranchera?*" I was often in the kitchen helping my great-grandmother prepare chile colorado, tortillas, frijoles, and arroz for the meetings taking place in the house. I traveled to San Francisco to attend a statewide MAPA (Mexican American Political Association) meeting with my dad when I was about eight years old. I remember sitting in on countless strategy sessions and political meetings. I was good at being quiet, and I was fascinated by all the activity and the significance of what seemed to be happening.

I remember listening to my mom and dad speaking to relatives and friends about the lawsuit against the school district, and when they finally made my dad a principal of the worst school in our district—the continuation high school. It didn't have its own campus, was housed in trailers on the main high school campus, and had a record of failed student after failed student. I remember listening to my dad brag and kind of "stick it" to his colleagues when he succeeded in having a brand new high school built with state-of-the-art equipment and a handpicked teaching staff. After years of struggle, that continuation school experienced great success, was given numerous awards for its various programs, and eventually had a stronger college entrance rate than the main high school.

My mom and great-grandmother also had a strong presence in the community and in our family in those years. I remember being stopped in grocery stores, at the bank, and on the street by strangers asking me to thank my mom, dad, or great-grandmother for something. Both my mom and dad were able to hold full-time jobs because my great-grandmother lived in the house with us and helped to raise my two sisters and me. The Chicano activists at that time always were grateful to eat some of "Grandma's" cooking during their visits to our home. Both my mom and my great-grandmother could play the traditional role of cooking, serving, hosting, and caring for the kids. However, they both were very strong, opinionated, and active women. I remember when a group of eighth graders participated in an essay contest about their hero, and the local newspaper contacted our home because an overwhelming number of the essay participants wrote about my mom, who was their teacher in some previous year. My mom was a teacher to many of the migrant farmworker children. She held them to extremely high standards and was known as fierce, loving, and able to produce excellence. Many of her students are teachers today.

While my mom and dad were fighting the world for educational access and civil and human rights, my great-grandmother was also engaged in very purposeful and strategic education of her grandchildren. My great-grandmother and I shared a bedroom. Late at night, while she was subversively smoking a cigarette, she'd tell me to pray for my mom and dad and for Muhammad Ali—a family hero. "Listen to your parents, *mija*, and learn from them. They are changing the world, just like that boxer." She would tell me stories from her own life about when she helped the "colored" children in her community. But I distinctly remember getting a rare scolding from her when I spoke meanly about the administrators that would not promote my dad. She told me to love those people and to pray for them. "We are supposed to love them, *mija*. Love and pray for those men so that they can do the right thing for your father."

Because I was an extremely shy kid, I could not imagine being a lawyer. Lawyers were strong, smart, brave, and vocal. Aside from my mom and great-grandmother, my heroes were exclusively vocal men. I was very proud of my dad, Cesar Chavez, Martin Luther King, Malcolm X, and Muhammad Ali. When Ali spoke with pride about being black, about winning his battle against the U.S. government when he refused to go to Vietnam, and when he excelled in the ring, all of us in my household were beaming with pride. We took what happened to Muhammad Ali personally, as if it were happening to us. We identified with his defiance and pride and the repression that he faced. He had a whole Chicano family feeling pride in his words and rooting for him.

I was exposed to two lawyers growing up. My dad served on the board of directors of the California Rural Legal Assistance and through that experience he got to know Cruz Reynoso. Later, when Cruz became a justice on California's Supreme Court, he would sometimes visit the Coachella Valley to speak at an event and my dad would take me to listen to him. I heard Cruz Reynoso speak about social justice and about how lawyers have a duty to society to contribute. Both Cruz Reynoso and Louis Flores gave me a skewed view of what lawyers and law were all about. I assumed that Cesar, Martin, Malcolm, and Muhammad Ali were all "lawyerly." I thought that both my parents and my great-grandmother were very lawyerly.

So, on the one hand, it seemed that I should become a lawyer. On the other hand, it seemed to be a position for only some very strong, confident, and vocal men.

Today, I am a lawyer. I almost want to write, "Technically, I'm a lawyer." That's because I have since learned that my understanding of what is "lawyerly" is not by any means a universal view. I don't feel like a lawyer in the traditional sense. I'm not necessarily interested in the practice of or the art of law for its own sake. A more honest description of who I am professionally is that I'm a leader-educator-manager-organizer-lawyer, in that order.

I obtained my law degree from UC Berkeley's Boalt Hall School of Law. When I first entered Boalt Hall in 1987, I had the hopeful expectation that this institution was going to teach me how to be effective in the social justice movement. I soon learned that legal education is not about social justice. In the law school curriculum, we were not going to learn about the civil rights movement, human rights struggles, the farmworkers, or how to build the movement.

It took me a long time to understand what we were learning. It felt like there was a great puzzle being laid out for me called "legal reasoning." I love puzzles, but as hard as I studied and prepped, I was not "getting" the game of law and legal education. Often, in the cases we were reading, there seemed to be no point, or worse, the judges and their legal decisions were surely wrong! However, I did not get truly demoralized until the first recruiting season at Boalt Hall when employers came to interview us for summer jobs. I was resisting understanding what law and legal education were about. But when I learned that the employers coming to recruit us were not anything like Cruz Reynoso or Louis Flores, I felt it like a punch in the stomach. The employers coming to recruit us were from law firms that definitely did not seem to be focused on the civil and human rights struggle. I felt stupid. Were my family and I the only ones in the world who did not already know that this is what law is about? I felt cheated. "What the hell am I doing here?" I thought to myself. My dream of becoming a lawyer and my parents' pride in my attending Boalt Hall suddenly seemed foolish.

Thankfully, something happened in that first year that helped me get over my feelings of alienation and demoralization. Someone distributed an article written by Duncan Kennedy in all of the mailboxes of first-year law students.[1] The article was a critique of legal education, of "legal reasoning," and law schools' failure to be relevant to the interests of disenfranchised groups in society. This article gave me a language and new framework for understanding my legal education experience that was not self-defeating and demoralizing. Oddly enough, though it was a critique of law schools like Boalt Hall, the article freed me to finally enjoy and tackle my legal education. My memories of Cruz Reynoso speaking in the Coachella Valley had new meaning for me. I took him to mean that no matter what legal education is supposed to be about, we have a duty to contribute to our community.

I became politically active at Boalt Hall in the diversity movement, which was at the time taking place at many institutions of higher education. Instead of having self-defeating inner talk about how stupid I was for not realizing what law was about, I became involved in a political struggle to make legal education relevant to the civil and human rights struggle. Making law relevant to social justice and to our communities is a thread that is constant in my work to this day. In my remaining years at Boalt

Hall, I experienced success in the traditional and not-so-traditional courses. I became politically active in challenging the institution, and I learned a lot about organizing and mobilizing for change. Ultimately, I truly enjoyed my legal education after all.

Upon graduation from law school I went to work at the law firm of O'Melveny & Myers. I had no misconceptions about what this was. I knew I was not working at a social justice institution. I chose this job because I feared being unemployed after law school, and nonprofit social justice institutions were not hiring inexperienced new graduates. Also, I wanted to know what those big law firms were about. I wanted to demystify it for myself. While there, even though I knew I would not stay in the firm for long, I made the best of it. I took on pro bono cases that were meaningful to me, participated in discussions within the firm about minority retention and diversifying the bar, and I engaged in volunteer work in the community. However, I was extremely unfulfilled, and my unhappiness showed. As soon as I learned that I passed the California Bar Exam, I began aggressively hunting for meaningful work. After O'Melveny & Myers, I began only working in areas of the law that inspired me. I worked on educational equity issues at the Office for Civil Rights of the U.S. Department of Education, then at the Mexican American Legal Defense and Education Fund, and eventually at La Raza Centro Legal in San Francisco.

La Raza Centro Legal was founded in 1973 by a group of Chicano law students and volunteer lawyers who recognized that existing institutions, even within the nonprofit sector, were not meeting the needs of Latinos in the San Francisco region. In its early years, La Raza Centro Legal consisted of several law students struggling to provide legal assistance to the community on a volunteer basis with support from local lawyers. Today, La Raza Centro Legal has a staff of nineteen members and serves thousands of low-income individuals from throughout the greater San Francisco Bay Area each year. La Raza Centro Legal provides direct legal services in the areas of employment, housing, immigration, and senior and youth law. Also, La Raza Centro Legal has innovative programs such as the San Francisco Day Labor Program, the Women's Collective, FairCare, and INS Watch. These programs combine service provision with community empowerment.

I was extremely attracted to and intimidated by La Raza Centro Legal because the agency practiced an empowerment style of lawyering. I was attracted to it because I believed in it; I was intimidated by it because I feared that I would not be good at it, and I feared the conflict that comes from challenging institutions of power. Working at La Raza Centro Legal has lived up to and exceeded my expectations. I am overwhelmingly challenged at times, stretched, and forced to grow and learn. It is amazingly rewarding beyond what I had the capacity to imagine prior to working there. It is a magical place in which people are transformed, and working within a magic space is incredibly special. It is also the toughest job I have ever held.

As a lawyer, I now know that laws, lawyers, and the legal system are not necessarily useful tools in pursuing social justice. The legal system is not a just one and is not designed to protect the interests of vulnerable sectors of society. We can use the law and the legal system to work for justice, but it is at times a weak tool. I have learned that I cannot forget or be naïve about whom the legal system is designed to protect. After all, for the most part, using the legal system requires hiring a licensed and trained expert, a resource that many people can't afford. Also, the legal process can be slow and cumbersome. Imagine a homeless day laborer who worked for three days for someone and was not paid. He is owed $400. If he knows how to reach the employer, which laborers often do not, and the employer refuses to pay, he can file a claim with the labor commissioner. This can mean several months of waiting for a hearing date. In the meantime, it is up to the lawyer to try to keep in contact with the homeless client, who has moved several times and is constantly struggling to find food and shelter. The legal system does not work well in such circumstances.

We have found a more empowering means of pursuing these legal claims. La Raza Centro Legal takes day laborer wage claims—even if the claim is for very little money. But instead of representing the worker, we provide training and education to day laborers and domestic workers to be able to be their own legal support on these cases. Under the guidance of an attorney, the laborers conduct the client intakes for these cases, make the phone calls to the employers on behalf of the aggrieved worker, and often directly resolve the cases. When negotiating with the employer does not work and they are forced to file a claim with the labor commissioner, the workers also organize a picket of the employer's home, a tactic that was devised by them, not lawyers. For these actions, the day laborer who is seeking the unpaid wages is directly involved in all aspects of the organizing strategy with significant support from other more experienced day laborers. When a group of ten to twenty-five day laborers show up at an employer's home at 6 a.m. with picket signs and a TV camera crew, they are almost always able to resolve the wage claim on that very day.

This strategy requires willingness on the part of the worker. Staff members from La Raza Centro Legal attend these employer pickets as backup and support. Attending such a picket is considered a part of lawyering at La Raza Centro Legal. Our expertise is effective in creating relationships with day laborer leadership and local media sources. We are willing to provide support and be the focal point of conflict to provide support to the workers. We engage in trainings about legal rights and responsibilities during such a protest.

In its way, the law can be a powerful tool for social justice. A legal victory can be validating. When a court finds in favor of the interests of seemingly powerless communities, it can feel vindicating and powerful. Also, legal victories can make change. The court cases that invalidated the "separate but equal" doctrine were important to those fighting to declare their humanity. My dad still feels anger when he remembers the "No Mexicans. No Dogs" signs from his childhood. The declaration that all of us are equally human under the law was an important one. Yet, we cannot ignore the fact that most children attending public schools today attend segregated ones.[2] For me, the legal battle over segregation provides an example of the tremendous validating strength and weakness of legal strategies.

Not only is the law sometimes a weak tool, but also lawyers themselves can be ineffective in pursuing justice. As a lawyer, I have learned just how ineffective lawyers can be to movement building. In fact, they can actually hinder or harm a movement. Don't get me wrong: lawyers can be inspiring. After all, my parents relied on lawyers and the law to get my dad out of jail, to sue the school district, and to validate our basic civil and human rights.

Yet, I have also experienced how lawyers can be big wet blankets on movements for social justice. After all, lawyers are trained in the law, and in large part the law is designed to protect the interests of the very powerful. For example, it is the "law" that deems a segment of our community as "illegal" for entering the United States and working and residing in this country without legal permission. It is legal within our legal system for immigration enforcement officers to terrorize individuals and families by detaining and deporting members of our families who are not residing within this country with legal permission. It does not yet matter under our laws how much an individual contributes to their family, to their community, to our society, or to our economy. It does not matter the emotional toll it places on individuals and families to live with the label "illegal." It is the law that permits U.S.-based companies to freely migrate to seek the cheapest labor force, while at the same time preventing individuals from pursuing the best opportunities for themselves and their families.

When undocumented immigrants organize to eliminate immigration enforcement in our communities, you can count on a lawyer explaining to the leaders of that movement how their efforts are in vain because it is legal for immigration enforcement to enforce federal immigration law. Lawyers are trained within the limits of existing law—existing law that is often unjust.

My upbringing combined with my current understanding of the law have taught me that you do not need to be a lawyer to advocate for social justice. After all, my great-grandmother was not a lawyer. She did not even boast a formal education. My parents were both educators, not lawyers. Martin Luther King, Malcolm X, and Muhammad Ali were not lawyers.

I am very influenced by examples of communities and individuals who are considered powerless by mainstream society actually exerting strong political power. In the valley where I grew up, growers had all the power—economically and politically. At least, that's the way it had always been and the way it looked on the surface. Growers were in elected office, owned the land in the area, and were the respected leaders of the community. Farmworkers were able to challenge the growers' monopoly on prestige through organizing, creative strategizing, ally building, media access, and legal strategies. People who had previously lacked respect were able to exert political power and force the growers to change their behaviors and practices. This was a powerful lesson for me to witness as I was growing up. I found it hard to imagine a seemingly more powerless group—non–English speaking, poor, Latino or Filipino, immigrant, and often undocumented laborers. Yet, they were able to organize, exert political power, and have their demands met by the growers who were forced to the negotiating table.

I am also greatly influenced by my great-grandmother's capacity to love in the face of injustice. Her worldview is an example for me of transformative visionary leadership. It is not necessary, nor even wise or powerful, to base a movement on hating the oppressor. The farmworker struggle did not require hatred of growers. This doesn't mean that I never dehumanized the oppressive growers in my own heart. I did. But that is not where our true power came from. That hatred and dehumanization is not the font of our victories. There are many examples of this transformative visionary leadership. For example, Nelson Mandela's strong vision and courage to sacrifice and dedicate his life for justice is inspiring. But even more inspiring for me is his refusal to vilify or make his captors inhuman. This I find to be transformative in a way that some forms of community organizing and traditional forms of adversarial lawyering is not.[3]

Maintaining a humanistic stance is a huge challenge in my work today. We often find ourselves vilifying an exploitive employer, or viewing individuals working in unjust institutions (mayors, police chiefs, governors, employers, presidents, etc.) as inhumane, not human, the enemy, subhuman, morally inferior . . . you get the point. When we create that hate or vilification of the "other," we sometimes still experience short-term victories—such as recovered wages, a won lawsuit, a good settlement, or a forced change in policy. However, this attitude keeps our work in those moments from being truly transformative. In those moments, we might be going for the victory, but we're not creating a new world with less hate. When our work is truly transformative and powerful, we are creating something based on love, not hate.

Staying true to this idea is more than challenging. At times it feels impossible. How do we build day laborer and domestic worker organizing and power, how do we empower individuals, and how do we empower a movement? How do we do so in a way that is truly transformative? To what extent does providing direct services or the art of lawyering hinder or help our vision of creating a powerful world with an empowered community?

First, let me start with a confession. I do not know the answers to the questions listed above. I have ideas that provide me guidance. I have experienced a series of failures and successes that also inform my direction and our work. However, I am facing these questions every day in my work, and every day I am forced anew to struggle through to find direction. It is what makes this work so challenging for me, and also what makes it exciting and powerful. When it seems absolutely impossible, my dad will be one of the first people to remind me that truly powerful work involves accomplishing the impossible.

At La Raza Centro Legal, in our work with day laborers we have succeeded many times in creating a powerful new reality despite difficult odds. La Raza Centro Legal adopted the Day Labor Program in 2000. At that time, La Raza Centro Legal was one of the premier and anchor legal services agencies in San Francisco. We were about twenty-seven years old. We had been providing high-quality direct legal services to low-income individuals from San Francisco, San Mateo, Marin, Contra Costa, Alameda, and Santa Clara counties for many years. Our services included housing rights, workers' rights, youth and senior rights, and immigration law.

Our reputation was one of a solid and strong legal services agency that often demonstrated a unique style of lawyering by involving clients directly in the cases and in pursuit of justice. Our employment law team demonstrated this type of lawyering. We would involve the client, for example, in determining the strategies for how to best recover his or her unpaid wages. Because of how slow and bulky the legal system was, this sometimes meant picketing the place of business or home of employers who were unwilling to pay wages to their workers. This strategy often proved more appealing to clients because they were able to be active participants in the effort to regain their wages and because they were not forced to wait the months and months that it took to get a hearing before the labor commissioner.

Our youth law team also demonstrated a style of lawyering that went beyond traditional means of legal representation. Our youth law work often involves representing a young person in a school discipline hearing or representing a disabled student who is unable to access services necessary to ensure he has equal access to an education. Since youth and parent involvement in education is a key component to educational success, it makes perfect sense that lawyering in this field would seek ways of directly involving guardians and youth in any efforts to ensure educational equity and success. Our youth law work, therefore, requires working very closely with youth activists, violence prevention and gang prevention counselors, after-school programs, and parent-led coalitions such as the Coalition for Fair and Caring Schools (FairCare).

Through our participation in FairCare, for example, we work with youth and parents to identify policies and practices necessary to ensure good-quality education. One effort addressed the problems that arise when schools and police criminalize students, a policy that was practiced in some of San Francisco's public schools. Some schools were very quick to call police onto campus for discipline incidents, even if there was no issue of safety present. One school asked the police to address the matter of a group of eighth graders who pushed a group of girls in the hallway. Another school called the police onto campus when a fourteen-year-old boy was believed to have stolen a tape cassette from another student. These are certainly discipline matters and opportunities to educate young people. However, some schools were quick to turn these incidents into criminal justice matters, especially when students of color were involved. Our youth advocacy team organized with FairCare regarding this issue. Youth and parents successfully advocated for, negotiated, and implemented a policy at the San Francisco public schools, which outlined when and when not to involve law enforcement in school discipline matters.

Our Ojo a la Migra team (INS Watch) was La Raza Centro Legal's first foray into developing a project which offered no legal or direct services. This was a pure organizing project, which the staff agreed to create at a retreat in 1999. INS Watch was formed to bring together immigrants, including undocumented immigrants, and allies of immigrants to challenge and resist INS enforcement activities. We named the project INS Watch because we were modeled after Bay Area Police Watch, which was created by the Ella Baker Center for Human Rights to address police abuse in the Bay Area. We wanted to be able to address INS abuse, eliminate INS enforcement in the area, and build bridges among different communities (immigrants and non-immigrants, Latinos and African Americans) regarding the issues of law enforcement abuse and activities. INS Watch successfully worked with immigrants in Windsor, California, to create a policy which would prevent police from cooperating or participating in INS enforcement activity. INS Watch also successfully organized immigrants and their allies to pass a resolution in San Francisco declaring the city an INS Raid Free Zone. These efforts served as a model for immigrant rights activists in other cities and counties throughout California.

INS Watch's membership at the time included domestic workers, day laborers, other immigrant activists, and nonimmigrant allies. The day laborers in our group provided a significant amount of leadership and added to our already strong relationship with the already established Day Labor Program and its constituency.

In 2000, La Raza Centro Legal became the umbrella agency for the San Francisco Day Labor Program. Adopting the program was, in some ways, a stretch for our agency, and in other ways it was a perfect fit. It was a stretch in that we are viewed as a legal services agency; the Day Labor Program is a job development and social service program for immigrant laborers. It was a perfect fit because our organizing work often had day laborers at its heart; they most often provided the leadership and vision to our work. On the legal services end, our agency already practiced an open-door policy for all day laborer cases. This meant that no matter how small the claim, we would provide direct legal representation to the laborers who were not paid.

Day laborers are primarily undocumented immigrant workers—usually men—who seek work by standing on public sidewalks in places where contractors and other employers can pick them up. In San Francisco on any given day there are approximately five hundred to eight hundred workers standing on streets seeking work. The City of San Francisco funds the Day Labor Program to address their needs. About two hundred men go to the Day Labor Program daily to seek work and other social services directly through the program. Some of these workers overlap with the workers who seek work on the street. Others only seek work through the Day Labor Program. The program also operates a women's collective. This is a group of predominantly Latina immigrant women who seek work as domestic workers and child care and adult care providers. While they do not typically seek work by standing on public sidewalks, they consider themselves women day laborers and part of the Day Labor Program.

The San Francisco Day Labor Program provides job development and other social services and facilitates community empowerment. We provide a safe and dignified place for day laborers to find work. However, given the huge number of day laborers in San Francisco, we do not find work for all workers daily. The program provides about four thousand jobs annually to day laborers. This results in about one job every three weeks to any worker who signs up on our list. We also provide direct services beyond jobs, including free legal representation, English classes, vocational training, mental health counseling, HIV/STD testing and counseling, a medical clinic, occupational health and safety training, literacy classes, life-skills classes, and clothing and food referrals.

The San Francisco Day Labor Program facilitates empowerment by providing a meeting space, creating community among the workers, operating a program run by and for day laborers, engaging in leadership development and organizing training, and implementing an agenda set by day laborers. Day laborers have set the following agenda over the past few years: (1) expand employment opportunities; (2) pursue immigrants' rights to have driver's licenses, (3) defend day laborers' rights to stand on the street free from police harassment; (4) pursue access to public restrooms that can be used by day laborers; and (5) create a site for the Day Labor Program that is accessible to the workers.

Because La Raza Centro Legal currently operates the San Francisco Day Labor Program, we are the first point of contact for complaints from or about day laborers. In San Francisco, the complaints that we often hear about day laborers include: they urinate in public, they scare away customers, they are "illegal" immigrants who don't belong here, they impact pedestrian and traffic safety by their presence on the sidewalks, they create too much trash, they are dangerous criminals, they bring down property values, they are disrespectful to women. These complaints are important in that they often lead to repressive policies against immigrant workers, they are barriers to creating community between immigrant workers and others, and they dehumanize day laborers and their experiences.

We also hear many complaints from day laborers including: there are no public restrooms available to them, they are treated with hostility by passersby and local residents, they are not paid for their work, they lack access to shelter or affordable housing, they face police harassment, they experience the fear of the local community, they suffer from loneliness and depression, and they desperately need more jobs. The women members complain about exploitive employers, fear of immigration enforcement, the challenges of raising families, their feelings of loss of children or family members who were left behind in their home countries, sexual harassment, domestic violence, and the desperate need for more jobs. These complaints are important because they may define what services day laborers need, are sometimes in line with complaints about day laborers, and can help create agendas and priorities for our work.

In San Francisco—depending on the economic conditions, the political administration at the time in the city, and the level of organization among immigrant workers—day laborers have been met with outright hostility, disdain, neglect, or support. At times, the city has tried to eliminate the public presence of day laborers by ticketing or harassing workers for standing on the street, ticketing or harassing employers who try to hire day laborers, or encouraging or forcing day laborers to stand in more remote areas looking for work. At other times the city has tried to create more helpful solutions to the day laborers' needs: creating access to public restrooms, increasing employment opportunities, increasing housing opportunities, and funding social services for day laborers. At other times, the city has attempted to create task forces or community forums to bring day laborers, local homeowners, and others together to address the "problems" created by day laborers or the "needs" of day laborers.

At La Raza Centro Legal, one of the principles that we most seek to implement and adhere to is that those most affected by injustice must be at the forefront of any effort to obtain justice. This means that the day laborers must set the agenda and determine the strategies. For example, if day laborers are ticketed for standing on a public sidewalk seeking work, they must be in the leadership of any efforts to challenge this practice. This principle is not always easy to accomplish. We have to overcome our own resistance and that of our colleagues and constituents to promoting and genuinely following indigenous leadership. For example, day laborers often assume that we at La Raza Centro Legal will have the magic answer for how to resolve their problem. It is sometimes surprising for day laborers when we encourage them to take the lead in resolving the issues they face. After all, even I sometimes wish I could sit quietly like I used to as a child and let the "grownups" decide things. There is something secure about having decisions made for you. While it is not empowering, it is nonetheless comforting at times—even when you do not like the decisions being made. There is something threatening about determining and taking responsibility for your own destiny and exerting it publicly. This problem is magnified when people are very poor, don't speak English, and are undocumented.

To be empowering in our relationships with day laborers, we have to invest the time and energy to bring workers together, providing education and guidance on what we as lawyers are capable of doing while at the same time brainstorming what the nonlawyers will also be able to accomplish. We have to overcome the temptation to usurp or co-opt leadership. For example, when we offer our opinion in day laborer meetings, it is sometimes treated as having more weight than that of the day laborers. If we show enthusiasm for an idea, the day laborers are more likely to rally behind it. If we are unsure or displeased with an idea, it usually gets voted down.

If I really think that we should move in a direction, I know that due to my position as the "licenciada" or the "directora" my opinions carry a lot of weight. I know that I can likely sway the group in a certain direction—not always, but I do have significant influence. So my challenge is to be conscious of this power dynamic, not pretend it doesn't exist. It often means that I withhold my comments and that I have to be extremely conscious of the words that come out of my mouth. It holds me up to a standard of speaking with integrity. I do not by any means always succeed at this. After all, I am only human. And I have not always had my ideas or direction approved by the majority of day laborers either. I've had the frustration of witnessing day laborers reject my "great" ideas.

When I slip up and try to take over the brainstorming or agenda-setting process, I might succeed at getting my way but I am not creating a world in which day laborers have power. If I keep my eyes on the prize—re-creating the world— then I am better able to avoid co-opting or usurping leadership. It is far more powerful, long lasting, and transformative when day laborers effectively advocate for their own interests in alliance with professionals, instead of depending on professionals.

As professionals, this sometimes means that we have to accept decisions that threaten our own comfort level. Indeed, at La Raza Centro Legal, I have my own comfort level challenged regularly. I really faced this challenge when day laborers who were being ticketed by the local police were organizing to challenge and resist this practice. Day laborers met with the police to explain their needs and their First Amendment rights to stand on the city's public sidewalks. This did not curb the police harassment of day laborers. The workers, after several meetings with the local police, then organized a town hall–style meeting with local political representatives from the board of supervisors. While they obtained the support of these members of the board, it did not put an end to the ticketing. When day laborers finally met with a representative from the mayor's office, they were told that the ticketing of day laborers was a policy that was fully supported by the mayor. At that point, the laborers decided to hold a public protest of the local police captain and the mayor. At that time the mayor's office was the largest funder of La Raza Centro Legal's Day Labor Program, and I knew that such a protest might trigger a response that could negatively affect La Raza Centro Legal.

This issue of funding is tough one. At La Raza Centro Legal, we are faced with the reality that the funding we receive to provide direct services to day laborers may be challenged by day laborers' organizing. Providing the services that day laborers need requires staffing which is expensive—especially if we are trying to live up to our principle of paying a living wage to our own staff. La Raza Centro Legal lost its funding from the city as a result of the protest held at the mayor's office. While we maintained our program and the services we were providing to the workers, the entire agency's staff took significant pay cuts and we laid off about one-third of the staff. There is nothing easy about following the decisions and direction of indigenous leadership. Yet today, day laborers are free from police harassment and ticketing as a result of that campaign. Even more important, the laborers themselves run our Day Labor Program—a leadership that was created by our commitment to facilitate and follow indigenous leadership. Finally, as a result of day laborer-led activity, the new mayor has committed to at least five years of funding for day laborer services.

Another important principle in our work at La Raza Centro Legal is that the agency must be what we are trying to achieve. We can't fight for workers' rights and be hostile or unjust to our own workers. We can't empower the community and ourselves be disempowered. We cannot seek to eliminate hatred against our community and ourselves engage in hateful speech or tactics. We cannot seek to humanize immigrants by dehumanizing others.

This simple principle is also extremely challenging for me. On good days it is easy to abide by, but what about when times are lean? What if you cannot afford to pay your workers a living wage? How do we as nonprofits live up to our principles in a world where financial support for our work seems to be so scarce? What am I doing to create that scarcity? In my role as executive director, I struggle with these questions daily. I have cut salaries, laid off staff, hired staff, promoted staff . . . all at different times as a means of seeking to create a safe, loving, and just work environment. There are times when I firmly believe that we have created this environment. But I have often failed. It is not a static process. From one day to the next, funding can be cut, an emergency can occur, a staff member could leave, or needs could change. I am constantly relearning that creating a healthy and just working environment is not a goal but an ongoing, staff-involved empowerment struggle and process.

Similarly, how do we humanize immigrants in a context in which they are treated with far less than humanity? Our government now interchanges the word *immigrant* with *terrorist*. Some local residents are quick to label human beings as *illegal*. I have not always succeeded at humanizing the individual who wants to tell me that "Mexicans do not know about personal hygiene." Like most people, when I feel angry or attacked, I often actively dehumanize individuals affiliated with the oppressive behavior or policies. I have relished, for example, in the public humiliation of government employees, police officers, and local residents who implemented policies that hurt day laborers or who I have labeled as racists. When I have been quick to label them as *anti-immigrant* or racist, it quite frankly felt good. Yet, in those moments, there is no hope for community between us. In those moments, I play a role in having day laborers become further polarized and viewed as the enemy.

Thankfully, I am learning. I relearned my great-grandmother's powerful lesson of love from a day laborer in our neighboring community of Oakland. In that community, day laborers were being referred to as *terrorists, thieves,* and *child molesters.* This hateful speech was perpetuated by a local politician and was generating and fanning the flames of fear in local residents. A day laborer challenged this dehumanization while refusing to dehumanize those who were attacking the day laborers. He went door to door speaking to merchants, local tenants and homeowners, principals of local schools, and even local Parent Teacher Associations that were vocal about their fears of day laborers. He talked about his own family, the children in his life that he was struggling to support, and the loneliness, joys, fears, successes, and failures that he was experiencing. He listened to them with compassion about their concerns and fears. Through his efforts, day laborers in Oakland gained some powerful allies in the local community—from the very same people that had previously been referring to them as child molesters! Together with their allies, they are challenging unjust city policies that adversely impact them.

Doing this work is extremely resource intensive. For example, having day laborers run La Raza Centro Legal's Day Labor Program means that some things are not as smooth as they could be. It requires seeking additional funding for training and professional development. Some of my staff members are struggling to learn English. Others are dealing with recent experiences of being homeless and on the streets. Staff members trained with a university or law school education have to learn how to organize and facilitate leadership. Providing day laborers with training and education about how to prevent lost wages or how to negotiate with employers is far more resource intensive than just simply having the legal professional file the wage claim. Yet, investing in day laborer participation is ultimately more effective.

At La Raza Centro Legal the lawyer's or professional's role may be to listen carefully to the issue at hand, ask many questions, and be upfront about the role we intend to play, the role we could play, and the role that non-lawyers could play to resolve the issue. It might mean explaining the legal process to a client and then pursuing a case on behalf of a client. However, it just as often may mean providing access to meeting space, paper, telephones, press numbers, allies, and meetings with representatives within in-

stitutions of power. It might entail being a point of access in an organizing effort. This could include learning and teaching the process of obtaining march
permits, making picket signs, or being in the photocopy room making copies
while the workers continue meeting and strategizing. It might mean babysit-
ting while the women's collective meets. La Raza Centro Legal staff members
are learning how to be effective teachers, how to demystify the law for themselves and others. We have to learn about effective marketing and media
messaging. Our staff struggles with learning about power, how to create it,
and how to challenge it. La Raza Centro Legal is an unusually challenging
place to work, and also a magical place of learning and creativity.

In doing this work, I find that I, my staff, or our agency are at the center
of conflict and often angering very powerful institutions and individuals.
The pressures can feel immense in those moments. We have received bomb
threats and hate mail and have been publicly picked on in the press. We
have lost funding and struggled with the internal conflicts that this can
cause. Yet, when I have been under some of the most intense pressure from
City Hall, I have had reminders from the community that I am supported.
When homeless individuals, youth in schools, or others go out of their way
to say, "Hang tough, I'm with you," those moments feed my courage and
help me to not lose hope. Fruit and bread have been donated to our offices
by impoverished day laborers when they learned that we were laying off
staff. Workers have donated significant portions of their humble wage claim
victories to help keep our programs operating. When, in the midst of the
mayor's retaliation, we no longer had funding to provide the day laborers at
our site a morning breakfast of coffee and bread, the workers began taking a
collection to provide this service themselves. I am humbled and inspired in
those moments.

What are the implications for me personally in doing this work? I am
alone and am in community. My allies are usually not other lawyers. When I
am among lawyers, I often feel alone. At times I feel that I have many
bosses—a staff of nineteen, a board of directors of ten to twelve people, and
the twenty to thirty day laborers and domestic workers who were elected to
represent the group as leaders. Many people hold me accountable. Recently
I was "summoned" to the weekly day laborers' meeting because they wanted
to address three things with me: (1) they wanted a financial accounting of
how we have budgeted and expended city funding; (2) they wanted me to
hear concerns they have about the effectiveness of our job creation efforts;
and (3) they wanted to express the need to do more effective marketing for
job development. In the same week, I was struggling to analyze whether we
could continue to maintain the same size staff or if we would need to make

some personnel cuts. By no means is this an easy job. This is not uncommon and keeps me on my toes.

In my work I strongly believe that the ends do not justify the means. However, I am often pressured by professionals who seek to convince me that we cannot pursue the agenda set by immigrant clients because it is "unreasonable" or "nonstrategic." When INS Watch, for example, decided to pursue a campaign that would end INS raids in San Francisco, I received many phone calls from colleagues, including civil rights advocates, urging me to not pursue this campaign. It was not strategic, and after all, the law permits INS raids. In those moments, I have to try to explain that the means of pursuing indigenous leadership is so important that we will not back down from it to try to accomplish a short-term gain.

Another example of this tension is when strategy meetings led by community members (day laborers, youth clients, immigrant parents) feel rough around the edges. They are not always linear as we are trained to think in institutions of higher education. Sometimes, the voice that comes from our constituents does not sound "sophisticated." I have to overcome the temptation in those moments to speak for our clients or the community. I am tempted because I sometimes suffer from the impression that my facility with the English language, organizational linear presentation skills, eloquence, or ability to engage in "professional" speaking will better serve our goals. However, I have to remind myself that excluding voices because they are not sophisticated enough does not build community power. Besides, in my experience, the voices of those most affected by an issue are always far more charismatic or eloquent than mine. I constantly relearn that I cannot exclude poor people from my strategies with the goal of creating a world that includes poor people. I have to walk the walk.

I have also learned for myself that the fear of repression is very real. I am not immune to it. In my work, I have to overcome the fear of conflict, failure, and humiliation. I used to be ashamed to admit that this fear exists. But now I know that it is helpful for me to share my own fears with others. It is part of creating access to the community. It helps in my work to explain, for example, to a client about the conflicts or retaliation that might ensue, about my own fears, and about how I intend, nonetheless, to overcome the fears to move forward. It demystifies leadership for our constituents. They are not lulled into thinking that leadership comes from fearless people. Leadership comes from everyday, ordinary people who have very real fears, who don't have all the answers, who might fail, and who nonetheless muster the courage to overcome those fears. It takes fear and courage to risk failure, engage in conflict, challenge power, and love people. There is no sense in pretending otherwise.

My personal experience at La Raza Centro Legal has been a challenging one. I have been at the center of much conflict and the target of much anger. I've read in the newspaper accounts from the mayor about how I don't know what I'm doing. I have worked excessively thankless long hours. I have had the humiliation of failing publicly numerous times. I have set out to reach ambitious goals and have had to acknowledge to staff and board members when they were not met. I have come face to face with my own weaknesses as a leader, with skill sets that I lack, and have known moments of genuine despair and fear.

I have also been overwhelmingly blessed. In trying to create a transformative space at La Raza Centro Legal, I myself have been transformed. I have discovered in myself that, in fact, that shy kid from the Coachella Valley is a leader and a lawyer. I have learned that while I acknowledge that the law is unjust, I can work to create justice as a lawyer. In struggling to bring an empowerment methodology to others, I have challenged myself to model and demonstrate empowerment. I have relearned over and over again that social justice is not a grandiose, elusive concept for us to accomplish someday. I have learned that to accomplish justice, I have to be just in all aspects of my being—in organizing at a large scale within the immigrant rights movement, in personal interactions with clients, constituents, or staff, and even at the most personal level with family and friends. There is no arena too small or too large. I have learned that while I sometimes fail at it, I am capable of creating power and social justice every day, in big ways and small. I have learned of the deep reserves I have of patience, humility, and courage. I have become integrally involved in a beautiful community of immigrant workers. I attend doctor's appointments, baptisms, and birthdays. I have been complained to, pushed, pulled, and taken care of by a huge community of immigrants, low-wage workers, youth, and their parents. I continually tap into the strength of my parents and sisters who are still an active part of my life. I am also part of a large community that is always growing, changing, and full of challenge, conflict, and lots of love. I have the experience of laughing out loud every single day. I am surrounded by powerful people who help me to learn how to create a new world.

While I am not in every moment able to tap into the understanding of what is possible—every once in a while, sometimes when I am not expecting it, I am able to truly believe and understand that absolutely anything, including the impossible, is possible. My goal and challenge for myself is to realize this more and more every single day. Justice is possible and I get to be part of it every day. What a miracle!

Notes

1. Duncan Kennedy, "Training for Hierarchy," in *The Politics of Law: A Progressive Critique*, ed. David Kairys (New York: Basic Books, 1998).

2. See chapter 3 in this volume.

3. The humanistic role of law in social justice movements was also well explained by Martin Luther King Jr. See his "Letter from Birmingham Jail" for the classic statement on law and social justice.

~

CHAPTER THREE

Organizing Education: Academic Research and Community Organizing for School Reform

Michelle Renée, Jeannie Oakes, John Rogers, and Gary Blasi

> We believe that research is key to the work that we do. As we try to advance an agenda around education justice we want school officials and elected leaders to understand that we know the data, we have access to it, and we'll hold them accountable.
>
> Luis Sanchez, InnerCity Struggle

Over the past two decades, activists have increasingly turned to organizing as they press for higher quality and more equitable schools in low-income communities and communities of color. To inform and make their campaigns credible, organizers have looked to education data and research for documentation of problems and evidence about potential solutions. Growing grassroots attention coincides with many researchers' disappointment at the failure of more conventional education reform strategies to blunt racial isolation and inequality in public schools. This convergence of interests between activists and researchers has prompted a handful of university-based research teams to ally with activist groups of young people, parents, and community members. For the activists, the alliances provide access to data and research that inform action. The alliances also increase the social and cultural capital of organizers as they gain access to funding and the policy connections of education researchers. For researchers, these alliances provide a site for participatory action research or "design experiments," where real-world problems and issues inform research agendas. Regular interaction and learning from the communities most impacted by educational inequality not only improve access to data but also inform the development and relevance of education theory. While the ultimate goal behind building alliances between researchers and organizers is improving the equity of the education system, shared knowledge and work enhance the processes of both community organizing and research.

In this chapter, we use our work at UCLA's Institute for Democracy, Education, and Access (UCLA IDEA) as an example of the theoretical and practical transformations that can result from such collaborations. We begin with a quick illustration of the persistent educational inequality that defines the context of both education organizing and education research in California. We then offer a theoretical critique of traditional school reform efforts and explain the potential of new collaborations between organizers and researchers. The center of the chapter provides a detailed discussion of our work building the Education Justice Collaborative (EJC)—a loose alliance of researchers, community organizations, and advocacy groups working toward increasing equity and improving the quality in California's school system. We conclude with a discussion of the added value that these collaborations bring to both organizing efforts and the enterprise of research, and we illustrate this value with examples from our activities over the past three years.

The California Context

Once heralded as the best education system in the nation, California's public schools now lack the resources needed to provide students with a quality education, and they are rife with inequality. California has adopted rigorous content standards, to which both textbooks and teacher certification are aligned, and students are regularly assessed on standards-based tests. High-stakes consequences—up to and including state takeovers and reconstitution—have been implemented for schools not showing progress on state assessments, and the State has threatened students who do not pass the required high school exit exam with the denial of their diplomas. Yet, the State does not provide the basic resources and learning opportunities necessary for schools or students to have a fair shot at meeting these goals.

National data comparing California to other states corroborate this dismal reality. Ninety-two percent of California schools spend less per pupil than the national average when cost of living is taken into account. Eighty-five percent of California's students attend schools in districts that have fewer teachers per student than the national average. Ninety-four percent of California's students attend schools in districts that have fewer counselors per student than the national average.[1]

Making matters worse for low-income children and children of color, the resources and learning opportunities that are available in California are distributed unequally across the state. California's low-income students, students of color, and English-language learners bear the burden of the inequality. Data we gathered for a statewide report of educational opportunity in California show the stark disparities.

> California's schools with the highest proportions of students of color, low-income students, and English Learners, are more likely to be overcrowded and poorly resourced than other schools in the state. A 2004 state-wide survey of over 1,000 California teachers revealed that schools serving 90–100% students of color are 6 times more likely than majority white schools to experience multiple opportunity problems—lack of credentialed teachers, high teacher turnover, poor facilities, and inadequate instructional materials.[2]

These serious problems of both education quality and inequality led to litigation in 2000, *Williams v. California*.[3] The settlement in 2004 brought unprecedented attention to the inadequate conditions in schools across the state. The *Williams* plaintiffs argued that students were not equally being provided even the basic learning resources (textbooks, qualified teachers, and safe, functioning school facilities). Interestingly, the State never once tried to suggest that these gross inequalities did not exist in California. Rather, the defense tried to argue that these basic learning resources were not necessary to increase student test scores and denied any responsibility of the State to address any deficiencies that did exist.

Williams proved to be a useful focus for education activism. Throughout the case, groups lobbied the governor, the state superintendent of public instruction, and the state school board to settle the case. Many members of the Education Justice Collaborative groups, especially students and parents, were witnesses in the case. The EJC groups also provided the media with examples of problems in particular schools and the ways those problems limited students' educational opportunities. Once the case settled, EJC groups campaigned to ensure a good faith implementation of the decision. Some are testing California's new uniform complaint process as they try to improve conditions in particular schools, others are monitoring their school's access to textbooks and other essential resources, and others are documenting implementation patterns across the state. While *Williams* began to make a dent in the gross inequalities, it remains only a small step in the right direction—educational inequality still persists in

California, as does organizing and advocacy on behalf of low-income students and students of color.

The Limits of Conventional Reform

Our interest in organizing as a strategy for reform came from our study of the limits of effecting change by implementing new educational technologies or structures. Though we strongly believe that research plays a role in education reform, our studies of the persistence of inequality despite interventions from the court, policymakers, academics, and other elites provide us with a more humble theory of change that acknowledges the limitations of research as the impetus for significant reform, particularly reform that seeks equity.[4]

Historically, school reforms have been based on a series of assumptions about the education system, the role of research, and American values. First and foremost are the assumptions that the education system is fundamentally fair in its provision of educational resources and opportunities and that different students achieving different outcomes is a result of meritocracy (if you work hard, you will succeed). Thus, inequities in achievement are placed either on the individual who does not succeed or on the system that had a design flaw that can be fixed. As a consequence, most reform attention is paid to fixing those system design flaws, such as improved curriculum or pedagogy.

Another widespread assumption among reformers is that lack of knowledge about a problem leads to inequality. Thus, if one found the root cause of inequality and then developed and implemented a technical solution, the inequality would disappear. For those operating on the deficit belief that students are at fault, a series of special programs for students in need, extra funding for schools, and even out-of-school services for families have been proposed. For those that understood a more systemic problem—the legacy of legal segregation or systemic funding inequities—remedies like desegregation plans and the equalization of state funding formulas were proposed. But these plans assumed that once the problem and solution were identified, America's commitment to equality would ensure they were implemented. The assumption is that racist practices are at odds with core American values, and once a racist practice has been identified (such as intentional segregation or racial inequalities in access to essential resources), the public will naturally move away from such practices. Instead, after decades of well-planned, well-intentioned reform, America's schools still provide dramatically unequal educational opportunities to its young people.

Traditional school reforms have focused primarily on the technical aspects of school policies (i.e., structures and practices), assuming either that the system is already fair or that practical solutions based in research will motivate well-intentioned schools to redistribute opportunities and resources equitably. Court-ordered reforms, less sanguine about "good intentions," have assumed that remedies designed by experts, most often researchers, will compel equity. However, neither of these strategies has accounted sufficiently for the intense political climate around schools,[5] and the underlying normative beliefs and implicit stereotypes[6] about race, class, and intelligence held by teachers, administrators, and parents[7] that sabotage equity reforms. The most formidable barriers to equity reside not in technical problems but rather in the cultural norms and biases regarding race, merit, and schooling that underlie the status quo and, for many people, make specific equity reforms so difficult to accept. Because privilege and exclusion are not discrete problems that result from ignorance but are rather the product of ideologies and cultural practices that are part of the foundation of our education system, technical solutions to education inequity will always fall short. Though having well-researched knowledge can inform a policy or reform effort, opposition to the political and cultural forces that maintain inequality must also be part of a successful strategy that challenges the status quo of power and privilege.

Community organizing, in contrast, has an explicitly political focus and does not shy away from directly confronting deficit assumptions about low-income students and students of color. The question that guides our work at IDEA is whether these explicitly political and cultural perspectives from community organizations could be combined with the technical expertise of research to create a better method for addressing the barriers to equity-focused school reform.

Our question is not whether researchers can become effective political organizers but rather whether they can accept that technical knowledge is only one part of the larger struggle for equitable schooling. How can researchers play a role in generating reliable, rigorous data to inform a larger public debate? How can allying with community organizers improve the quality and relevance of the research that is produced? In convening the Education Justice Collaborative, we realized that our expertise and comparative advantage lay in studying, analyzing, and reporting data; in assessing systems of accountability and the effects of particular changes in educational practice; or in surveying public attitudes toward education. We also realized and accepted that the growing community of education advocacy and activist organizations are better equipped to use the information to influence the political and cultural debates on behalf of those with less power in the education policymaking arena.

Increasing Involvement of
Community Organizations in Education

The *Williams* case and other evidence of the crisis in California schools have increased the number of community organizations and advocacy groups engaged in education reforms and policy. In our 2005 survey, we found sixty-four organizations actively working on educational equity in California alone.[8] This high level of involvement is seen nationally as well: a 2001 study identified more than two hundred grassroots groups across the United States engaged in campaigns for educational justice,[9] and anecdotal evidence suggests that far more groups are organizing today.

Some of these organizations are focused solely on education issues, while others work on multiple issues. For example, ACORN (Association of Community Organizations for Reform Now), PICO, and IAF (Industrial Areas Foundation) have recently become more active on education issues after years of organizing and building considerable political power in campaigns for living wage jobs, affordable housing, health care, and other social goods. Because this high level of engagement of community organizations in education reform is new to the academic literature about both education and social movements, we provide below a brief glimpse into this growing phenomenon.

Researchers investigating education organizing for school reform have described how parents, youth, and/or neighborhood residents engage together in collective action directed at winning concrete improvements at the individual school level, in school districts, or in state and federal policy. Their work most often targets unequal resources, power, and learning opportunities. Some campaigns focus on a single school or education policy, and many others nest schooling problems into larger problems in society and the economy. The more expansive view places schools at the center of the community, and hence at the center of changing inequity in the large social and political economy.[10]

Community organizing as a reform strategy directly challenges conventional forms of school-based parent involvement that only ask parents to support school decisions and practices and work within the existing power structure. Community organizing also challenges the power relations that underlie failing schools and communities.[11] This new type of involvement not only addresses particular educational problems; it also changes the role of low-income communities of color in shaping state and local policies. In this way, such organizing serves the dual role of improving education directly and increasing the social capital of communities.[12]

Preliminary evidence suggests that, in many places, community organizing is successfully transforming education policy and increasing the democratic participation of low-income communities and communities of color.[13] As one example of the changes that take place at an individual school site, Shirley (1997) documented that, in the neighborhood surrounding one Texas school, IAF organizing led to the closure of vacant buildings where drugs were being sold, an increase in funding for an after-school program, the development of community policing, the development of an integrated housing strategy that supported low-income tenants, and the empowerment of parents to meet with local government officials and participate in public meetings.

Similarly, a study of twenty-nine different community organizations working on education reform in California found that, across the state, community organizations can have an impact both at the school site and in the larger community. Organizations were successful in improving the safety of school facilities, increasing support for student achievement, and increasing the equity of school and district policies and practices. Researchers also documented increases in the representation of youth, parents, and community members on the school board and other decision-making bodies. Through activism, organizations developed the skills of key leaders and engaged a base of members for both local organizing and a statewide movement. Taken together, sustained organizing led to an increased awareness of educational inequality and the community capacity to advance an equity agenda.[14]

Similarly, a study of the Industrial Areas Foundation in Texas found that community engagement in education reform led to the development of more racially inclusive, and politically effective, democracy.[15] Simply put, building power to transform schools also builds power to create more inclusive and democratic communities. Though the most obvious goal of organizing is changing education policies and practices, the examples above demonstrate that organizing for education issues is intrinsically linked to increasing the social and political capital of low-income communities and communities of color.

Studies of community organizing for education reform emphasize that organizations need allies and that they are wise to build strategic alliances with researchers and other experts. For example, studies of community organizing in Texas emphasize that campaigns benefit from leadership development activities allowing community organizers to directly engage researchers and intellectual leaders in studying the new issues and developing policy options and strategies.[16] Other studies briefly mention the importance of using research as a strategy for informing problems and solutions, developing a campaign, and persuading supporters and opponents.[17] However, the intersection of education research and organizing has not been thoroughly explored in academic literature. We know little from the existing literature about how groups identify the information they need, access existing research, relate to researchers, or actually use research. Thus we created the Education Justice Collaborative with the idea that research could play a constructive role as advocates and organizers become more involved in education reform, but part of our experiment has been to figure out what that role may be and how it may work.

The Education Justice Collaborative

The Education Justice Collaborative is a loose coalition of approximately thirty student, parent, educator, and advocacy organizations. Some of the grassroots and advocacy groups have worked together in the past; others have not. Some have prior experience working on state policy issues; others have been engaged only in local activism. These very different groups agreed to collaborate because they thought it might increase their chances of success. Although the specific goals vary among the EJC groups, each hopes to create schools that provide all students with a genuine opportunity to graduate from high school ready for college, meaningful work, and full participation as members of a democratic society. There are too many groups involved in EJC to describe all of them here, but we introduce a few of our partners in this section to provide a glimpse into the diversity of organizations that make up the EJC.

Many of our partner organizations are local or regional groups of parents and students that focus their work on a particular school, school district, or region. For example, InnerCity Struggle describes its organization's mission "to promote safe, healthy and non-violent communities by organizing youth and families in Boyle Heights and East Los Angeles to work toward economic and social justice."[18] Among many successes, InnerCity Struggle ran campaigns to build three new schools in its community to relieve overcrowding and allied with other Los Angeles organizations to make college preparatory coursework the default curriculum for all high schools in Los Angeles Unified School District. InnerCity Struggle has achieved such ambitious goals by employing a multilayered organizing strategy that includes community organizing, leadership development, education and training, media advocacy, and alliance building. As it engaged in this work, InnerCity Struggle has called on IDEA researchers for various data needs, including assistance in developing survey instruments for action research among its members, generating reports of state data that document overcrowding, and presenting education research that shows the promise of providing all students access to rigorous coursework.

Parent U-Turn is another local EJC partner. Focused on building the power of parents in the Lynwood School District near Los Angeles, Parent U-Turn uses accountability as the framework for its organizing. In the following passage, Parent U-Turn members articulate their mission and goals.

> Parent-U-Turn (PUT) is a community organization that provides training to other parents to make them knowledgeable about the educational system. PUT has built parent power that creates change. PUT has advocated for bottom up accountability as a strategy for a new form of parent involvement in holding school officials accountable for providing decent conditions and meaningful opportunities for students in urban schools. PUT has engaged parents in workshops for making sense of performance standards, high stake exams, learning standards and the conditions necessary for urban students to navigate through the public school into college.

> PUT work is based on the belief that since parents have the most stake in schools, they should have the greatest voices in governing them. Because of their unique commitment to their children's education, parents are less likely than teachers or researchers to be compromised and more likely to demand and work to achieve high academic standards.[19]

Though centering the importance of engaging parents directly in school reform, Parent U-Turn has also been strategic in building alliances with researchers and others. IDEA developed extensive research training programs for Parent U-Turn, shared critical data about school inequality, and helped facilitate Parent U-Turn's connections to other organizations working on statewide reform. As a result of this alliance Parent U-Turn has been able to garner some of the social capital that is often only conveyed to elite academics at universities.

EJC also includes statewide education justice organizations. Californians for Justice (CFJ) grew out of student activism against anti-immigration and anti-affirmative action propositions in the 1990s. Now a large grassroots organization with five regional chapters and a state office, CFJ has been working on campaigns to increase the opportunities that low-income students of color have to learn, including active work against the California high school exit exam and ensuring fair implementation of the *Williams* settlement. CFJ explains its mission:

> We bring people of color, young people, and poor people together by leading large-scale community education efforts, training a new generation of grassroots

civil rights leaders, and mobilizing public support for major public policy change in California. From the street level to the state level, we are building a society based on the principles of racial justice, human rights, and full participation.[20]

Working with EJC allows Californians for Justice to maximize the power of its campaigns. It turns to EJC partners for grassroots support and research. As one example, later in this chapter we describe the Education Opportunity Reports that IDEA created in response to a request from CFJ.

EJC partners focus their work on many issues, not just education reform. Many are affiliated with national organizations that forward a comprehensive social justice agenda. For example, ACORN uses its powerful infrastructure and reputation to tackle school reform in northern and southern California. With over twenty-four thousand low- and moderate-income member families, California ACORN is the state's largest community organization focused on the rights of low-income families. Like our other partners, ACORN has requested research support from IDEA. As one example, IDEA researchers and ACORN organizers in Oakland worked to develop a program to increase the number of credentialed teachers in the schools that come from the local community.

In addition to these local and state grassroots organizations, EJC includes a number of advocacy organizations that are focused on legal and research strategies. Lawyers at Public Advocates, the ACLU of Southern California, and other civil rights organizations have played an important role in advancing the educational rights of students in California. Through the *Williams* lawsuit, these lawyers successfully argued that all students deserve access to basic educational resources. Because the EJC organizations needed solid research about educational inequality in California, IDEA researchers investigated the *Williams* plaintiffs' claims about horrific schooling conditions in which low-income students and students of color were expected to learn. Some of the results were used in expert reports prepared in conjunction with the case, and they were disseminated widely to community groups in accessible pamphlets. Since the settlement of the *Williams* case in 2004, IDEA researchers also worked with EJC partners to assess the implementation of reforms required by *Williams* and to identify areas needing further work.

Employing different strategies, the organizations engaged in the EJC explore two propositions collectively: (1) A high-quality, equitable education system in California requires fundamental and systemic state policy changes, and (2) such changes cannot be achieved without the engagement of an educated and activist public. The EJC also acts on the premise that, to achieve equity, policymaking and policy implementation must confront the "common sense" cultural norms behind current inequities, alter the existing distribution of resources and political power, and find solutions to the problems that currently pervade the system, solutions that are informed by research and are relevant to communities.

Each EJC group—grassroots community activists, advocacy organizations, and researchers—brings different strengths to the collaborative work. Some of the grassroots groups have a large, active membership base, the political capacity to organize state and local campaigns, and knowledge of the school systems that comes from the students and parents that form their base. The EJC advocacy groups that do not have a membership base engage in legal and political advocacy on behalf of low-income communities and communities of color. Some have long experience in navigating the state capital and in the courts. The researchers and staff from UCLA IDEA bring the capacity to conduct rigorous and relevant research on issues related to grassroots campaigns and advocacy and have access to technical expertise in key areas such as policy development and working with the media.

Together the EJC has negotiated a careful balance of collaboration—knowing what expertise each group brings to the dialogue and acknowledging when it is time to let other experts lead. EJC activities provide a forum for regular learning interactions. Community organizations inform the collaborative about key issues in regional areas; policy advocates offer regular updates about the current debates in the state capitol. The EJC forum also provides a venue for the activist groups to identify shared interests in particular issues and find areas for joint political action. The synergy among the groups makes the EJC a site in which different organizations maintain their unique identity while learning from one another and building collective power.

The hope behind UCLA IDEA's participation in the EJC is that activism to increase the equity of California's education system can be bolstered by access to relevant and rigorous research. As researchers, we join EJC in dialogue about the problems and strategies for achieving potential solutions. As we do, we learn a great deal about the community's perspective on education issues and about activist reform strategies. IDEA generates research products (including reviews of existing research and new analyses) that respond to questions posed by the grassroots and advocacy groups. And, as the groups use research as part of their activist strategies, we also learn more about political relevance of academic research. While our primary goal in working with the EJC is to infuse relevant research into education organizing, we know that our research has improved by engaging with community organizations. Having regular meetings with people in the field means that we know what research topics are relevant to current policy debates. Interaction with community organizers also means that we get regular updates about how a particular policy is being implemented around the state. Such real-time information helps us develop relevant research products and informs the development of the theories we use to guide our work.

How Does the Education Justice Collaborative Work?

Since the EJC is rather unique, it is worth sharing the logistics of the work we do: how EJC is staffed, the different components of our work, and the value that we believe this work has to the endeavors of creating more equitable educational opportunities in California.

The EJC is designed to create the space to exchange ideas and information. It is not an organization that initiates or runs campaigns. UCLA IDEA's team of senior scholars, postdoctoral fellows, graduate students, and professional staff with expertise in education reform, community organizing, politics, policy, and communications work together to ensure that the EJC has the logistical support for deliberations, meetings, and other opportunities for participants to work together.

Initially, many of the community-based groups, youth organizations, and civil rights advocates had reservations about working with university academics. Not surprisingly, some were suspicious that the university was too entrenched in the status quo. Others worried that academics would "pull rank," dominating discussions and forcing their own agenda. Each organization wanted to maintain its autonomy and ability to choose which projects to engage in. Building trust was a long process that involved meetings, conference calls, and slow ventures into joint work. Establishing clearly defined roles as well as relationships that go beyond those formal roles also helped solidify the partnership.

Over time, the EJC project has grown not only in the number of participating groups but also in the policy issues of collective interest and in the types of joint activities it engages in. Policy issues include educational funding, teacher quality, adequacy of facilities and instructional materials, supports for English learners, high-stakes testing, college access, the nature and availability of educational data, and multiple conceptions of education accountability. EJC joint activities are of four types:

1. generating and sharing rigorous, accessible, and useful research and data analysis about the current status of California schools and about the potential impact of alternative policy options;

2. building alliances and joint projects among a wide range of grassroots groups, advocates, reform-minded educators, civic organizations, and researchers;
3. developing participants' capacity to engage in public policymaking arenas;
4. developing participants' capacity to engage media in ways that build public knowledge as well as the political will for adequate and equitable schools.

By simultaneously developing these four different types of activities and relying heavily on the collaborations among the many organizations engaged in the work, the project gives a broad array of Californians access to the resources, expertise, and opportunities for participation in democratic decision making. We describe each area of work in more detail below.

Research and "Research Translation"

Providing research to education activists is not a linear process in which the researcher locates a question, conducts a study in the community, and then disseminates the results. It is better to think of the process of producing relevant research as a symbiotic relationship: both researchers and organizers have different resources, knowledge, and needs, yet both need each other to succeed in improving the education system. The relationship needs to be built, nourished, and challenged to continue to grow. The rewards and demands can be immediate and long term. With this in mind, the research strategy of the EJC includes producing research on demand, developing new data-based reports, and hosting education exchanges, workshops, and one-on-one coaching to build capacity to use existing research and generate new research.

Research on demand includes quick analyses on questions that are pressing to our community and advocacy partners. The research on demand can be relatively simple. For example: "How do Los Angeles high schools vary in their college preparatory course offerings?" or "How does Oakland's teacher shortage impact students in different neighborhoods?" Answering such questions involves queries and recalculation of publicly available state data. But other questions are more complex and involved: "Does a teaching credential mean a teacher is qualified?" or "How can multiple measures of inequality be used to calculate the schools with the most need?" These questions force us to engage the academic literature, look for researchers whose expertise lies in the particular area, or build new statistical models for quantifying educational opportunity. IDEA attempts to provide accurate, timely, and accessible answers to these questions. Unlike most academic settings where analyses and deadlines are flexible and "generalizable" results are provided to peers, activist community allies usually require timely analyses that are specific enough to make an impact in policy deliberations and accessible enough to be understood by the public.

While quick data-based answers to specific questions are enormously helpful, activist groups also need and want deeper, research-based analyses of education issues. Using both traditional and innovative strategies, we also produce accessible data reports based on available national, state, and local data. For example, to explore the relationship among schooling outcomes and educational opportunities, we have juxtaposed California's schools' Annual Performance Index scores and college-eligibility rates with school characteristics such as teacher quality and provision of college preparatory curriculum. We have also explored the relationship between schooling opportunities and demographics like the student racial and social class composition of schools. The reports of our work may take the form of easily read text; a map made using geographic information system (GIS) software; a series of charts, tables, and graphics; or, as in most cases, a combination. To place numbers and statistics in context, these reports also synthesize the finding and policy alternatives that have been published elsewhere in education research.[21]

As one example, we developed a report series titled "California Educational Opportunity Report 2005." The opening for this report arose after a meeting between our partners at Californians for Justice and Jackie Goldberg, the chair of the California Assembly Education Committee. The organizers and chair realized that members of the education committee needed more specific information about how denying diplomas to students who did not pass the high school exit exam would impact students in their districts. Both the chair's legislative staff and our organizing partners contacted us and asked us to provide information on how many students were at risk of failing the exit exam in each legislative district.

After discussion with the EJC groups, we realized that information could also be useful to organizers across the state, particularly if we developed a series of reports that put the exit exam pass rates into the context of the unequal educational opportunities provided to low-income students throughout California. The result was a set of single-page "reports" that displayed legislative district–specific data on teacher shortages, overcrowding, access to rigorous course work, school funding levels, and other school resources, alongside the exit exam pass rates that the committee chair had requested initially. The framing of the text, the data analyses, and the display of test score gaps in the context of educational opportunities were all grounded in previous, respected scholarship and careful new analyses, yet the reports were presented in a colorful, simple, and easy to follow format.

Our UCLA research team also has produced *research translations* of academic scholarship on issues of particular interest to the EJC groups. These succinct pamphlets define and document an education problem and highlight potential solutions from the research literature. Written in both English and Spanish, the pamphlets have been used in our partners' community outreach and leadership development activities. Some of the topics addressed include: shortages of qualified teachers; inadequate instructional materials; facilities problems; overcrowding; limited accountability; the failure to serve English learners well; and disparities in school.

We also convene "education exchanges" sharing research. The exchanges provide advocates, organizers, and members of community groups with the time to learn more about a particular issue directly from researchers. In the daylong exchanges, EJC participants and researchers share and construct knowledge together, examining academic research from the perspectives of community experiences. Past education exchange topics include: opportunity to learn, teacher quality, school finance, school facilities, and accountability.

Finally, we have also provided workshops and one-on-one coaching sessions that teach EJC participants to use publicly available databases and research and to conduct their own action research. The workshops have focused on developing specific research and advocacy tools—for example, accessing state education databases and using web-based GIS software to map education resources at local schools. One-on-one coaching allows us to help organizations with specific needs like developing surveys, analyzing data, and investigating the history of education problems.

Constituency and Coalition Building

Critical to making research relevant is providing the environment for collaboration to occur. The EJC provides a space not just for collaboration between organizations and a research institution but also the much-needed time and space for organizations to collaborate with each other. IDEA hosts monthly conference calls that allow everyone involved to update each other on campaign activities, funding opportunities, and long-term plans, as well as to synchronize events and the messaging behind shared issues. Weekly conference call "working groups" also focus on developing knowledge and policy options related to issues of joint concern. The working groups have explored issues such as estimating the real costs of providing high-quality education to all students, eliminating obstacles to equitable college access, and finding ways to make the high school diploma meaningful without high-stakes exit exams. By including a mix of researchers, organizers, and advocates, the working group meetings always bring multiple sources of knowledge to bear on the task of identifying problems, formulating strategies to expand public awareness, and generating ideas for policy solutions.

We have also developed http://justschools.gseis.ucla.edu, a website for expanding and supporting the network of community-based organizations. The website includes the different research products discussed above, shared definitions of the problems and solutions to the education crisis in California, and links to the affiliated organizations. The website and monthly calls, combined with regular email contact and in-person education exchanges, help build cohesiveness and trust between the different research, advocacy, and grassroots organizations participating in the project. In addition to providing direct support to the organizers, the ongoing collaboration enriches both the quality and the relevance of the research we produce.

Capacity Building

It is not only information about education that the community and advocacy organizations are interested in but also insights into the formal processes and rules of legislation and the informal practices of the state capital hallways and chambers. Although insider groups are acquainted with the processes by which principles and policy are transformed into law, regulation, and practice, these processes are not clear to many important constituents. To remedy this imbalance, we help groups learn to navigate California's policymaking apparatus with relationships, tools, protocols, and field experiences that build knowledge, skills, and confidence. For example, our partner, attorney Elizabeth Guillen of Public Advocates, designed and taught a workshop on the nuts and bolts of Sacramento education policy. Each participant was given a workbook with background on key legislators, the overt and covert steps by which a bill becomes a law, and tips for how to hold a successful meeting with a legislator. After a morning of lecture, participants were given the unique opportunity to practice what they learned in mock sessions with former legislative staff and elected officials. These kinds of activities are one of the ways we have tried to make a conscious effort to transfer the social capital usually conferred on university researchers to the community organizers with whom we work.

Media Communications and Public Engagement

Increasing public understanding of the nature and extent of the problems confronting K–12 education, the systemic factors producing those problems, and the feasibility of systemic reform requires both accessible information and a reframing of the discourse about public education in California. EJC engages in research with communications professionals using polling and focus groups to explore the contours of public opinion about public education (i.e., how important sectors of the public think about the problems of K–12 education, and how they can be better informed and engaged in solutions). Based on this research, we work with the EJC groups and the media to give wide visibility to activities of community organizations pushing for reform.

Our media strategy includes assisting organizations in getting coverage of their work and campaign issues; providing organizations with media training; and providing daily briefings of state media coverage of education equity. We have a full-time media director who coordinates a comprehensive effort to increase the press coverage of the organizations' work. This includes assistance in framing press releases and opinion pieces; training in working with the media; support in building relationships with reporters; and workshops on creating framing and messaging. In addition, a second full-time media staff person prepares a daily briefing on education justice issues in newspapers around California. Called "Education News Roundup," this useful tool is emailed to organizers and researchers around the country.

What We Have Learned: The Richness of Joining Forces[22]

The descriptions above highlight some of the tangible goods that the EJC aims to provide to community organizations. Yet another layer of analysis is worth exploring—the larger lessons about the power of joining research with community organizing to bring about positive change in California's schools. In this final section, we explore the dynamic nature of the collaboration between research and organizing, focusing on the different uses and forms of research, and the value that collaboration adds to community organizing, research, and ultimately the struggle to increase the equity of the education system.

One of the first things we noticed in working with community and advocacy organizations is that we have multiple understandings of what counts as research and what makes research relevant to the organizing process. To examine this idea, a team of IDEA researchers conducted interviews both internally and with community partners.[23] Compare the contrasting expectations about the purpose of research between IDEA researcher Joanna Goode and Parent U-Turn organizer Mary Johnson.

Joanna Goode: As an academic, I view research as a process of identifying some intriguing problem or question about a given situation, developing some theories about the issue, conducting a methodologically sound study guided by these theories, and finally, disseminating the results in a way to solve the problem.

Mary Johnson: Research for my organization is information on conditions around schools. Conditions such as where our schools lack textbooks, lack of credentialed teachers, bad facilities, and discipline problems that are not addressed. Our schools have high levels of suspensions, and poor communication with parents. They lack bathrooms or if they have bathrooms they are locked. These are the things that we need to document and bring back to the district to show the conditions in our schools.

Following the scientific method, researchers are trained to begin with an observation, investigate existing theory, design a methodology, study the problem, and then propose solutions. Research, under this definition, emphasizes the procedure of generating new knowledge as much as, if not more than, the final product. With our community partners we notice that the emphasis is placed first on the product—the data that will be immediately useful to inform their specific concerns. These understandings of research are not mutually exclusive. Rather, collaboration between researchers and community activists requires a both/and approach. When trying to make research useful to the organizing context, research must both follow the utmost scientific rigor and center the perspectives and needs of the community being studied.

Similarly, the purpose of research must be thought of as both advancing the larger body of knowledge about an issue and solving specific, current problems. Collaborating with community organizations does not mean that scholars need or ought to give up rigorous science or to stop engaging in the creation of purely theoretical or scholarly knowledge. Rather by continuing to use rigorous science while engaging with community organizations we find that we bring important contributions to academic knowledge—studies that are more directly linked to knowledge from low-income communities of color and theories that more accurately explain the problems and challenges of transforming education.

Another issue we have dealt with in our collaboration is credibility. What makes research credible in community organizing contexts? Again we have found multiple layers of understanding around this issue. Research needs to be credible both to the organizations and to the decision makers who are the ultimate audience for the data. Californians for Justice Regional Director Yvonne Paul describes these two different layers of credibility.

Academic research brings its own credibility and validity because that's the kind of research we are conditioned to value. Academic research is thought to be the pinnacle. But, I think the research that gets generated from sources that are known to have similar social justice, human rights values has a greater credibility with our constituents. The research that is credible to our constituents is research that validates our experiences. There's a lot of research out there that invalidates our experience like research from folks on the [political] right. It's really important for individuals to see a broader context so they can start to dismantle some of the internalized oppression that folks carry with them.

Paul explains both that academic research is held in high regard in the political arena and that research that comes from a social justice perspective is particularly valuable among her organizations' constituents.

As researchers we have found that maintaining our credibility with decision makers, the media, and other academics is based on ensuring that our methods and analyses follow the highest academic rigor. We find ourselves doing twice as much work in order to successfully engage with community organizations—we continue to stay current by publishing and engaging in our own field but also add another layer of work to make basic research skills and solid research-based knowledge available to our partners. It is important to emphasize that maintaining our credibility with community organizers is also based on our willingness to engage as a partner with organizations rather than solely as a proprietor of research. That is, our willingness to listen, learn, and sit at the table is as important as the rigor of our research.

Our partners have also taught us that, at times, it is far more powerful to the organizing process for research to be generated by the community and advocacy organizations themselves. As Mary Johnson from Parent U-Turn explains:

> I think that the research Parent U-Turn does gets more respect [from school district officials] because they know that we are people from Lynwood, South Gate, or LA. They know that we're doing research and they know that it comes from people within the community. And they know that Parent U-Turn has the connections within the community, with the churches, with schools that can support this information. Our research is more than a number on the chart; it represents a real person.

Our partners have used the process of conducting a survey, writing a report, or examining data as more than just a way to gather knowledge. The process of conducting research and owning the findings can be powerful in training leaders or developing a broader constituency around an issue. In these cases, research assistance from IDEA takes the form of advice on methodology and guidance in interpreting results. Such assistance is just as important as taking the time to turn our own survey results into an easy-to-read report. It is important to emphasize that the research done by community organizations has a different goal than traditional academic research—the findings are never meant to be sent to an academic journal. Rather, community-driven research may be intended to inform the leadership of the organization, demonstrate public opinion to decision makers, or identify education problems that need attention.

The multiple layers of legitimacy and credibility cannot be drawn with clear lines. It is clear that organizing efforts in low-income communities and communities of color are best served by multiple kinds of research. Luis Sanchez, executive director of InnerCity Struggle, explains this well.

> Researchers bring a wealth of information to the partnership. They're always finding new research that helps support the work that we are doing. IDEA can give us the answer to questions within a day that would take us two weeks to figure out. It matters, on some level, that we're working collaboratively with UCLA. When you're trying to move an equity focused policy agenda with both parents and students, a lot of them ask where this information came from. It helps to tell them that we've been working with professors at UCLA to show that it is something we haven't made up. . . .
>
> Yet we have the people that are most impacted by the system. Our parents and students attend schools that are underserved. When our members do research, they think through what questions would be key. In the end they are the ones that are going to have to push the agenda. It should be them, because they are the people most impacted by policy.

At IDEA, we keep this articulation of dual research needs at the forefront of our work. At times we can pull together a report or simple state data in a way that is time efficient and useful. Sometimes, our access to the critical social capital of foundations or decision makers is what is most valuable. At other times, community members are in the best position to ask the research questions and gain the most value from conducting the research on their own. The combination of maintaining academic rigor, engaging in the struggle, providing tangible research assistance, and respecting our role in the process forms the ethics behind our relationships with community organizations.

While supporting organizations in doing their own research, we at IDEA also conduct research independently. The goal of this work is twofold—both investigating answers to pressing questions that arise for our partners and adding to the larger body of knowledge on equity-focused education reform. The critical ingredient in establishing and keeping our credibility, in fact, is our insistence on analytic rigor and honest reporting, alongside a deep understanding of our unique role at the forefront of our work. We explore problems, solutions, and strategies with our partners, but we leave the political action to them. One of our primary tasks is to make complicated relationships and patterns more transparent and compelling to lay audiences. Though it can appear that some of our work is obvious and uncomplicated—for example, calculating frequencies from publicly available State data—the way we frame those quick numbers and analyses is based on decades of research. The other task we have is communicating the importance of the role that community organization can play in equity-focused education reform to our colleagues in academia, foundations, and the government. We explain each of these tasks in more detail below.

We think of our work as translating between the language of research and the language of activism, without misrepresenting the meaning of our analyses. The challenge is to transform theories and data into legible and relevant text and graphics. The Education Opportunity Report described earlier provides an example of this translation. We did not just create an Excel spreadsheet and post it on our website; neither did we avoid using numbers or complex educational theories. For example, the excerpt below describes inequities in education resources.

Resources in California Schools[24]
California schools spend less per pupil (after adjusting for cost of living) than almost any other state in the nation. As a consequence, California schools rank at or near the bottom (49th or 50th) of all states on a number of essential resources.

- 92% of California schools spend less per pupil than the national average when cost of living is taken into account.
- 85% of California's students attend schools in districts that have fewer teachers per student than the national average.
- 94% of California's students attend schools in districts that have fewer counselors per student than the national average.
- 98% of California's students attend schools in districts that have fewer librarians per student than the national average.

We presented a series of statistics in sentences that are free from academic jargon. By providing clear interpretations of the numbers, the sentences increase the likelihood that the information will be interpreted accurately. Though short, this report is still based on theories of educational opportunity. Research demonstrates that access to educational resources, including teachers, counselors, and librarians, is important to student learning and college access. Rather than an extensive review of the literature on this point, we use it to shape our presentation of the data. Further, the data sheet has a link to our website where organizers can access more detailed information on these topics. Our fact sheets and other data products attempt to transform carefully computed data and complex theory into clearly written points that are both accessible and accurate.

It is our hope that the research products we create and the time we spend sharing our knowledge of education research directly benefit our partner organizations. We have also sought to support their work in another important way: communicating the important role that community organizations can play in equity-focused education reform to our colleagues in academia, foundations, and the government. We believe that both our "expert" findings in this regard and the social and cultural capital that we enjoy as university researchers are helping to establish the legitimacy of grassroots organizing and community advocacy in the education policy process. Here, too, the support is not unidirectional. Our relationships with the groups have also heightened the credibility of our work and given it considerable visibility in low-income communities of color that would otherwise (and for good reason) be quite skeptical about researchers' assessments of their circumstances.

Behind all of this work is the truth that fundamental social change rests on multiple forms of knowledge.[25] Experiential knowledge that comes from living through the injustice of social inequality is especially valuable. We remind ourselves that our research interactions with the EJC are ones from which we, as well as they, can learn. EJC members' knowledge is essential to our understanding of the most pressing education inequity issues and in determining the research that best supports the struggle for justice. That is, working with community organizations has significantly enhanced the quality and relevance of our research. The EJC allows us to engage in a dynamic process in which research, action, preparation, and planning occur organically. There is no beginning, middle, and end of the project; rather, it is a relationship from which all of us continue to learn. Through these relationships we gain access to knowledge about schools, families, and young people that a traditional researcher who sends out a survey, conducts a few interviews, or spends a week or month observing would never access.

Being pushed to make our work easy to understand and relevant has transferred to our academic writing, teaching, and presenting. Learning to write for multiple audiences, designing compelling graphics, and communicating big ideas succinctly are skills that have made our academic work more accessible as well. The GIS maps, for example, are useful not just to policymakers but also to other education researchers who are trying to understand the context of a particular school or community. As another example, over the last five years, our community partners have presented with us at academic conferences. Their presence has sparked fascinating discussions and shifted more than one researcher's understanding of how educational inequality impacts low-income communities of color. While researchers are used to talking in the abstract about "those students" or "those parents," it is quite another experience to have a dynamic seventeen-year-old explain how the lack of qualified teachers at his school relates to patterns of systemic oppression.

At the core, respect is what defines our collaboration: respect for each other's roles, respect for our own contributions and limitations, and respect for the struggle for equitable schooling. Furthermore, the ever-present race, class, and power differences between researchers and low-income communities of color are acknowledged in our collaborations—especially because of our collective focus on race and class disparities. Those of us at IDEA reflect on our various forms of privilege, including race, class, access to political capital, access to social capital, and access to financial support for our work. We make a conscious effort to conduct our work in a way that recognizes rather than ignores these sources of inequality within our collaboration. In presenting grim statistics, we as researchers, each with different forms of privilege, acknowledge that in theory we can share outrage, though, in practice, some of us will never truly know how upsetting it is to hear that our child is at the lowest performing school in the state or that our child will not be able to get into college because our schools did not provide enough college preparatory courses.

Taken together, our research strategy means that we provide research to groups, train organizers to conduct their own research, and build bridges across organizing, academic, foundation, and policy arenas. The demands of organizing require such a multifaceted approach to providing research assistance. Successful collaboration depends on validating multiple forms of knowledge—and understanding what forms of knowledge are most useful in what kinds of situations. Working together does not mean that community organizers must become researchers nor that researchers must become organizers but rather that both groups can benefit and learn from each other.

The ultimate goal of our collaborative endeavor is to increase the education opportunities provided to low-income students and students of color in California. The remarkable organizations that we partner with are indeed making changes around the state. Californians for Justice succeeded in winning a two-year delay in implementation of California's high school exit exam and continues to work on state education policy. InnerCity Struggle joined forces with the Community Coalition and other Los Angeles–based grassroots and advocacy organizations to convince Los Angeles Unified School District in spring 2005 to make California's required college preparatory courses the "default" curriculum for all high school students. CADRE (Consortium for Appropriate Dispute Resolution in Special Education) organized teams of parents, community members, and students to test the *Williams* settlement complaint process; they worked with teachers and administrators to make sure that they took the necessary steps to fix problems. California ACORN worked to equalize low-income students' access to highly qualified teachers by influencing layoff policies in two urban school districts that were grappling with state budget reductions. These organizations put countless hours into their campaigns; they are the work of hundreds of low-income parents, students, and community members of color and their allies. Clearly these groups will transform the state without any help from a small team of UCLA researchers. But it is our hope that our work gave these groups better access to research and that this research helped inform and support their efforts to increase the equity of California's schools.

Notes

We collaborate closely in our work at UCLA IDEA. The work described in this chapter reflects the insights and labor of many of our colleagues. In particular, Julie Flapan manages the EJC team, Joanna Goode did much of the data analysis for the reports we describe, and Rocio Cordoba coordinates our media program.

1. J. Rogers and J. Goode, *California Educational Opportunity Report 2005* (Los Angeles: UCLA Institute for Democracy Education and Access).

2. Rogers and Goode, *California Educational Opportunity*.

3. *Williams v. California*, No. 312236. First amended complaint for injunctive and declaratory relief (Cal. Super. Ct. 2000).

4. J. Oakes and J. Rogers, *Learning Power: Social Inquiry, Grassroots Organizing and Educational Justice* (New York: Teachers College Press, 2006).

5. A. Wells and I. Serna, "The Politics of Culture: Understanding Local Political Resistance to Detracking in Racially Mixed Schools," *Harvard Educational Review* 66, no. 1 (1996): 93–118.

6. G. Blasi, "Advocacy Against the Stereotype: Lessons from Cognitive Social Psychology," 49 UCLA L. Rev. 1241.

7. J. Oakes, K. Welner, et al., "Norms and Politics of Equity-Minded Change: Researching the "Zone of Mediation," in *International Handbook of Educational Change*, ed. Andy Hargreaves et al. (Boston: Kluwer, 1998), 952–75.

8. M. Renée, J. Oakes, and J. Rogers, *IDEA Survey of California Education Organizations* (Los Angeles: UCLA Institute for Democracy Education and Access, 2005).

9. K. Mediratta and N. Fruchter, "Mapping the field of organizing for school improvement: A report on education organizing in Baltimore, Chicago, Los Angeles, the Mississippi Delta, New York City, Philadelphia, San Francisco and Washington D.C." (New York: Institute for Education and Social Policy, New York University, 2001); California Tomorrow; Designs for Change; Southern Echo: 73.

10. D. Shirley, *Community Organizing for Urban School Reform* (Austin: University of Texas Press, 1997); M. R. Warren, *Dry Bones Rattling: Community Building to Revitalize American Democracy* (Princeton, NJ: Princeton University Press, 2001).

11. Mediratta and Fruchter, "Mapping the field of organizing"; K. Mediratta, K. N. Fruchter, et al., "Organizing for school reform: How communities are finding their voices and reclaiming their public schools" (New York: Institute for Education and Social Policy, 2002). See also M. E. Lopez, "Transforming schools through community organizing: A research review" (Boston: Harvard Family Research Project, 2003); and E. Gold, E. Simon, et al., "Bringing Community Organizing into the School Reform Picture," *Nonprofit and Voluntary Sector Quarterly* 33 no. 3 (2004): 54S–76S.

12. C. Delgado-Gaitan, *The Power of Community: Mobilizing for Family and Schooling* (Lanham, MD: Rowman & Littlefield Publishers, 2001); Warren, *Dry Bones*.

13. Shirley, *Community Organizing*; Mediratta and Fruchter, "Mapping the field of organizing for school improvement"; Warren, *Dry Bones*; D. Shirley, *Valley Interfaith and School Reform: Organizing for Power in South Texas* (Austin: University of Texas Press, 2002); Gold, Simon, et al., "Bringing Community Organizing into the School Reform Picture"; K. Mediratta, *Constituents of Change: Community Organizations and Public Education Reform* (New York: Institute for Education and Social Policy, Steinhardt School of Education, New York University, 2004), 68.

14. M. Chow, L. Olsen, et al., *School Reform Organizing in the San Francisco Bay Area and Los Angeles, California* (Oakland, CA: California Tomorrow, 2001), 106.

15. Warren, *Dry Bones*.

16. Shirley, *Community Organizing*; Warren, *Dry Bones*.

17. See, for example, Mediratta, *Constituents of Change*, 68.

18. This information is from InnerCity Struggle's website, http://innercitystruggle. org/.

19. Personal communication, Parent U-Turn, 2006.

20. Information is from Californians for Justice website, www.caljustice.org/.

21. To find examples of this work you can visit the IDEA website: www.idea.gseis.ucla.edu/.

22. The quotes in this section come from our readers' theater presentation: J. Flapan, J. Goode, M. Renée, J. Rogers, J. Mendoza, J. Oakes, et al., *Outside the Ivory Tower: Research and Community Organizing for School Reform* (Montreal: American Education Research Association Annual Conference, 2005).

23. Flapan et al., *Outside the Ivory Tower*.

24. Rogers and Goode, *California Educational Opportunity*.

25. Oakes and Rogers, *Learning Power*.

~

CHAPTER FOUR

LULUs of the Field: Research and Activism for Environmental Justice

Manuel Pastor, Rachel Morello-Frosch, and James L. Sadd

Introduction

In the last two decades, the environmental justice movement has taken firm root in the larger struggle for social justice in the United States. Its origins lie in community resistance to the placement of various LULUs (locally undesirable land uses) in marginalized communities. One watershed moment in the movement's emergence was a massive protest in 1982 against the placement of a hazardous landfill in Warren County, a poor, predominantly African American community in North Carolina. The resulting arrest of five hundred activists and community members harkened back to the tradition of the civil rights movement and helped launch a national awareness of the tendency for environmental hazards to be concentrated in low-income communities of color.[1]

While mobilization and protest have been hallmarks of the environmental justice movement, the movement has since its earliest days combined straightforward activism with careful research. The Warren County protest, for example, triggered a study by the U.S. General Accounting Office that found that hazardous waste landfills in the southern United States were disproportionately located in black communities.[2] The United Church of Christ, a main proponent of organizing for environmental justice, commissioned its own research team that found that the location of hazardous waste and toxic disposal facilities across the nation was positively correlated with the proportion of residents of color.[3]

Research activities were not limited to the community or governmental side of the ledger: university-based researchers and other professionals also have been key to the movement's evolution. In 1990, for example, sociologist Robert Bullard, who had been working on issues of environmental racism in collaboration with community groups since 1979, published a landmark volume, *Dumping in Dixie*, that brought together case studies of both siting and community mobilization in southern black communities.[4] That same year, a conference on environmental justice, sponsored by the University of Michigan, brought together researchers, activists, and policymakers, laying the groundwork for both a major volume on the issue and a new commitment by the U.S. Environmental Protection Agency to create an Environmental Equity Working Group.[5]

While the decade and a half since has also seen the emergence of a more strictly academic literature on environmental disparity—including criticisms of the precepts of the movement to be discussed below—the pattern of engaged scholarship has remained a constant. Community–university partnerships have continued to spring up, so many of which are groundbreaking that we hesitate to name them for fear of failing to honor all the important actors in this emerging area of collaboration. For this chapter, we discuss our own specific collaboration with community groups in the area of environmental justice—in particular, a nearly decade-long partnership with California's Communities for a Better Environment (CBE) and a few other environmental justice organizations. As we will show, this collaboration has both led to a steady stream of research publications and helped to strengthen organizing and advocacy by those community groups seeking policy change.

In keeping with the themes of this volume, we discuss our work not to celebrate our own contributions but to elucidate the supportive role that research and other professional activities can play in community struggles. Because of the specific history of our evolving relationships, we think our experience may be somewhat different than others and thus may provide some unique lessons for those interested in the intersections of professional activity and social justice advocacy. In particular, unlike other academics, we generally have not really conducted "action research" projects, that is, research focused on specific sites or specific campaigns, such as an analysis of a particular land use or school cleanup.[6] While we have collaborated with community groups in determining research questions and designs and always worked to ensure that the research is relevant to emerging policy issues, we have instead primarily worked on a series of broad academic studies documenting environmental disparities in California that have been used to set the stage for more specific actions.

This focus on "framing" the debate seems to be all the rage in today's political environment, but this priority for our work arose due to a particular historical phenomenon: just as the environmental justice movement was gaining ground, a series of broad research studies (including Anderton et al.) were questioning the very existence of disparities.[7] Our initial effort, then, involved investigating and establishing the existence of environmental racism in Southern California, the place where we began our community collaboration. That such a broad research project resonated with the needs of community organizers, who are often characterized (usually from afar) as focusing on more immediate issues, speaks to both the vision of those organizers and the need for researchers to rethink their assumptions about, and relationships with, community-based groups.

We specifically suggest that while many assume that community groups only desire immediately "relevant" research and data analysis, there is also a demand for the sort of "fundamental" or field-shaping research that can shift the terms of the debate. Moreover, the usual notion among researchers is that engagement with community is likely to diminish or at least skew research objectivity and quality. Our partnership with community organizations has, to the contrary, enhanced the academic quality of the work. It has also had an important transformative effect on us as researchers in ways that have changed our style of work and production. Finally, it has ensured that our work has found a policy audience, getting at that elusive grasp on social change that so many researchers seek but find difficult to obtain.

This chapter lifts up these points as follows. We begin by detailing our own entrance in the environmental justice field as researchers, and we discuss how this led to a set of useful intersections with community organizers, especially those associated with Communities for a Better Environment. We then turn to the evolution of the working relationship with CBE, pointing out the rules—ones that honored both community control and scientific integrity—that needed to be in place to make our particular collaboration successful. We then discuss the challenges and differences that have emerged as we have tried to replicate the collaboration in a different geographic setting, raising issues of how transportable the initial relationship may or may not be. Finally, we conclude with some general lessons that may be of use to others considering or working within such community–university partnerships.

Getting to Know You: Common Interests, Uncommon Opportunities

Since 1996, we have (in different combinations) been involved in a series of research activities and community collaborations around environmental justice issues in California. Our primary partner, particularly since 1998, has been CBE, a statewide group that had traditionally focused on broad issues of environmental protection at the community level, often with a scientific bent. The organization has evolved significantly since its inception and has now become most identified with the environmental justice paradigm emphasized by its Southern California chapter.

That environmental justice would become salient as an issue in Southern California is hardly surprising. While there has been some degree of controversy in the research field with regard to the presence of environmental inequities, a series of studies, many of which were produced by our team, have seemed to suggest that "the Southland" is an area where the case regarding environmental disparity is in little doubt.

Indeed, much of the impetus for our collaboration from CBE emerged from an intersection of interests around the mixed evidence at the national level and the implications for Southern California. The early 1990s seemed to be a high-water mark for those concerned about environmental inequity, that is, the disparate exposure of minority and low-income communities to hazards and air pollution. As noted in the introduction, a pathbreaking study from the United Church of Christ had established that hazardous waste and toxic disposal facilities were positively correlated with the proportion of residents of color in the same zip code areas.[8] In 1991, the first People of Color Environmental Leadership Summit in Washington, D.C., produced a set of environmental justice principles, and, following up on the Environmental Equity Working Group established under President George H. W. Bush, the Clinton administration issued an executive order in 1994 mandating that environmental justice be considered by all federal agencies. Yet, just as momentum was being established in the fields of organizing and policy, a new wave of studies called into question whether the disparities existed at all.[9]

These studies made several technical points about the way studies of disparities should be performed. The first involved geography, with the critics arguing that zip code areas were the wrong spatial unit for considering neighborhoods and that census tracts, a more compact and socially homogenous geography derived from the census process, were more appropriate for finding patterns of disparity. The second point was that early associations of ethnicity and pollution in the literature failed to control for other factors, such as land use and income, which might explain the pattern. The income issue was especially important, to the extent that disparate exposure resulted not from racial discrimination but from market forces, such as the purchase of lower-valued land by either polluting industries or minority homeowners, then disparate outcomes could reflect impersonal "market choices." Progressives might object—differential income and land values are, after all, partly a result of America's racialized economic opportunity structure—but a finding that race was not important after controlling for income also meant at a policy level that civil rights law was not as relevant, and so one of the usual policy and legal leverage points for environmental justice might be eviscerated.

The early studies critical of environmental justice did make use of tract geography and suggested that race was not a significant determinant of hazard location, especially when one took into account the proportion of local residents employed in manufacturing industries, based on the hypothesis that firms might choose to locate near potential employees.[10] The fact that the waste industry would invest in research to counter the claims of environmental justice advocates suggests just how politically charged research agendas can be—and it also puts in context the charges of lack of objectivity that often face those researchers who instead choose to work with affected communities.

While some of those critical of the Anderton et al. studies were content to simply point to the funding sources, others launched a set of counterstudies and methodological criticisms, some involving highly technical issues such as the exclusion by Anderton et al. of certain areas (such as any tract in a metropolitan district with no hazardous facilities) from the analysis.[11] Activists also argued that these studies were biased because they were funded by a grant from the largest waste management firm in the United States, and an examination of some of the underlying research does suggest a particular packaging of results that minimized evidence of disparity.[12]

Our earliest work was among those pieces that actually decided to take the Anderton et al. approach seriously, particularly the shift to census tracts and appropriate controls for land use, income, and other explanations. We were particularly interested in the early 1990s in whether the results regarding environmental disparities (or their absence) would hold on a test of Southern California. We were convinced that the distribution of hazards should really be considered in the context of regional industrial clusters—that is, the furniture-making and metal-plating industries in Los Angeles were not likely to drift up to Seattle, and Microsoft was not likely to relocate itself in Hollywood, and so it was the relative equity of the distribution of toxics within a particular region that mattered.[13] This sort of bias against national-level studies and what they might hide was at that time more a premise than a proven fact, but a recent national study[14] has attempted to take on both the broad national picture and the local regional impacts by using statistical controls to see whether patterns of disparate impact exist region by region, that is, once one takes into account regional specificities of industries through what is called a "fixed-effect" regression strategy. The results indicate sharp disparities for both African Americans and Latinos, even after controlling for income and other variables, and lend credence to the notion of looking at a regional level for concrete patterns, effects, and possibilities.

Our first study was actually initiated by a set of undergraduate researchers who were both engaged by these methodological issues and interested in social justice; this reflects the sort of transformational work that this book is meant to inspire, although we must admit that we were as inspired and transformed by these plucky undergrads as they were by us.[15] We first looked at treatment, storage, and disposal facilities (TSDFs) for hazardous waste in Los Angeles County, exactly the topic (if not the geography) of the Anderton et al. studies. Our analysis found significant demographic differences between census tracts (or neighborhoods) with TSDFs versus tracts without.[16] In particular, those tracts hosting a TSDF or located within a one-mile radius of a TSDF had significantly higher percentages of residents of color (particularly Latinos), lower per capita and household incomes, and a lower proportion of registered voters.

We also utilized more sophisticated strategies to see whether race still mattered when we controlled for zoning or neighborhood income. It turns out that it does and, moreover, that income has a complicated effect: at the lowest level of income, there was a lower likelihood of being near a facility (perhaps because there was so little economic activity in the neighborhood at all), and at higher levels of income, there was also a lower likelihood of being near a facility (presumably because of high land costs and enhanced political power); and the likelihood of being near a hazardous facility actually peaked at what might be thought of as working-class communities of color. Our study also revealed a finding not usually explored in the literature: facilities in Los Angeles County were actually in areas of higher density of the residential population (once one controlled for the adjoining industrial land use and properly divided the population by the amount of usable land).

These findings, initially published in a news article in the *Los Angeles Times* in summer 1995 that highlighted the finding that minorities were three times as likely to live near a hazard,[17] spurred the interest of the Southern California organizers for CBE. They were, after all, seeking to move an environmental justice agenda with a series of communities that perfectly fit our research profile as most vulnerable: heavily Latino, mostly working class, and living in densely populated areas side by side with hazards in the heavily industrial Alameda Corridor. Mutual contacts after the article came out—and the controversy it caused, including the resulting call by the Los Angeles City Council for an Environmental Justice Task Force—indicated a possible interest in collaboration and actually built on an early set of political intersections around environmental organizing in the city of Huntington Park.

To understand CBE's interest in what may seem to be arcane and highly technical debates regarding proof of disparity, it is useful to understand its organizing model. Beginning in 1993, partly as a result of its increasing attention to the issues of disproportionate exposure of low-income communities of color, CBE began to pioneer a surprisingly simple model of environmental justice advocacy. Coined the "triangle approach," it combined three major tools employed by organizations working for broad social change: (1) community organizing that could inform, educate, and engage affected constituents to address social inequities through collective action; (2) science-based advocacy that would include independent scientific analyses to understand the consequences of disparities and policy actions; and (3) legal interventions that made use of government regulations and judicial rulings to change the behavior of private and public entities.

In CBE's view, most efforts to reform environmental policy had typically employed only two of these strategies: science-based advocacy and legal intervention. The result had become a sort of "dueling experts" model in which the community voice was left out and policymaking became increasingly the province of disconnected professionals. On the other hand, environmental justice advocates often had been successful at mobilizing communities but sometimes had been less adept at countering business-supported arguments being proffered as a way of derailing environmental progress. Expertise was needed, but many activists were wary of working with the mostly white professionals associated with mainstream environmental groups. In addition to making good use of its own staff scientists, CBE was looking to fill this technical breech.

The way the three pieces came together for CBE is perhaps best illustrated in an area of its work in which we were not directly involved: the so-called bucket brigades. The brigades were originally formed in 1996 by CBE in a "fenceline" community abutting a refinery in Richmond, California; the buckets were air samplers that community organizers could use after various refinery incidents. The use of these buckets as a focus of community organizing grew out of their initial deployment in 1995 to document emissions as part of a lawsuit against a Unocal-owned refinery.[18] Law, science, and organizing came together in a seamless trio, and it was exactly this sort of combination that CBE was also seeking in Southern California.[19]

The immediate target of CBE's concern when we came together was a health risk standard that had been adopted by the South Coast Air Quality Management District (SCAQMD) in the early 1990s. Used for regulating the cancer risks from existing facilities, the standard set the "threshold of significance" at a lifetime estimated cancer risk of one hundred per million for people exposed to a particular set of emissions. This standard was twice as high (i.e., less restrictive of pollution) as business interests had been requesting and ten times the level the professional staff had recommended. The more lenient standard had emerged partly because of the SCAQMD's fear that tighter regulations would deter investment in a Southern California economy suffering its worse recession in post–World War II history. Communities, on the other hand, were appalled by the standard, and environmental justice communities were particularly concerned about cumulative impacts—that is, the effects of having several facilities in proximity, all emitting multiple toxics that were individually "acceptable."

For CBE, this was an important issue primarily because it squared with an attempt by the organization to "scale up" its environmental justice efforts. It wanted to show that a regional approach might be one way to tackle the particular disparities in a series of neighborhoods and therefore build a more unified regional movement. But to get there, it needed studies, such as the one we had produced, that suggested that there was a regionwide problem of unequal exposure and therefore a sort of "commonality of disparity."

We, on the other hand, were interested in both expanding our work and, given the frightening pattern we had found, connecting with an organization that could actually move an agenda. Our sense was that despite whatever data we might produce, communities of color were often being ignored in public policy debates—and no study, no matter how sophisticated, could shift policy in the absence of political pressure. Given the absence of attention by elected and appointed officials, we understood that political pressure would have to be organized from the grassroots. In short, for our research to have impact, we needed community allies—just as they needed us to both connect the regional dots and provide backup for their arguments for community voice and environmental justice. This was an uncommon opportunity to find common ground—and thus, a research and activist alliance was born.

Building a Relationship: Developing
Trust and Negotiating the Rules

Our alliance with CBE was greased by an extraordinary act of fate. Part of our mutual courting was facilitated by Santa Monica–based Liberty Hill Foundation. Liberty Hill is an explicitly progressive foundation whose slogan is "Change, Not Charity," and its funding of activist groups is well known throughout the Los Angeles region. Liberty Hill had been acting as a particular sort of fiscal agent for CBE: when CBE secured a settlement as a result of lawsuits against polluters, it was generally prohibited by state law from recovering more than its legal and related operating costs. As a result, the settlement money would be given to Liberty Hill and the foundation would then distribute the funds to smaller environmental justice start-up organizations. Liberty Hill itself did not have significant resources, but it had played an important role in the social justice community in Los Angeles and was useful at brokering the first few meetings of the researchers and CBE leaders to establish our common base for working together. As these commitments to each other were being crafted, the California Endowment approached the partners—Liberty Hill, CBE, and the research team—to see whether we might be interested in financial support for our emerging collaborative.

Unsurprisingly, we were interested, and we wound up with a three-year grant of $1.7 million, with 27 percent of the money supporting the organizing work of CBE; 55 percent going toward training, secondary grant-making, and organizational capacity building to be coordinated by Liberty Hill; and the balance (18 percent) supporting the research team's work on air pollution and environmental hazard studies in Southern California. The grant was subsequently renewed at a lower level for an additional two years, and we collectively went on to leverage other resources for a study on children's environmental health and the expansion of the collaborative model to Northern California (a process that is in progress and is discussed below).

As a result, it was a relatively well-funded collaboration, but we would stress three points here. First, the collaboration grew out of interest and not funding. Indeed we are quite concerned about the viability of community–university collaborations that are responses to monetary opportunities rather than reflections of shared political commitments, because initiatives that chase after money tend to be short-lived, lacking in a community base, and unproductive. Second, both in the original collaboration and in subsequent funding incarnations, there has been a commitment to keeping the research portion below the other two shares of organization and training/start-up, partly to correct for the relative access to resources and to mirror the understanding that it is organizing driving the research and not primarily research "with an organizing face."

Our third point is that some clear ground rules about the collaboration needed to be established early on. The first of these reflects the last point made: We established a decision-making process in which any member of the collaborative could bring a research idea to the table but that ultimately CBE would be able to exercise veto power as to whether the idea was pursued with collaborative resources. This did not stop our own sometimes excessively technical forays in research—we have spent more time working at issues of spatial autocorrelation (that is, whether the clustering of certain people and activities affects the statistical significance of empirical tests) than might be considered mentally healthy! But it did mean that we generally pursued such topics with other funding streams and that the research produced through the collaboration dovetailed with a strategic organizing effort to change environmental conditions in Southern California.

The flip side of this—one also important to CBE but sometimes less consciously embraced when working with other community groups—was the need for respect for the scientific method. That is, just because a research topic was collectively chosen did not mean that the results were guaranteed to turn out a particular way. The most crucial example of this came when the researchers proposed that we utilize the data set on hazardous facilities to answer a question that had bedeviled researchers and policymakers alike: Which came first, the minority communities or the hazards? The issue has sometimes seemed more fascinating to researchers than to activists. From the research view, understanding the temporal dimension could give us more insight as to the processes that generate environmental disparities. Activists, on the other hand, sometimes argue that regardless of the timing, health hazards mandate regulatory action. But this question is also important for activists, partly because the idea that low-income minority communities just "moved in" is often used as a way to derail community calls for action and remediation. Moreover, there are implications for policy: whether we should focus on tighter controls on siting or provide more environmental information to renters and house-seekers depends on the answer to the question of timing.

When the research team proposed following up the original study that had triggered our mutual coming together with a study of "which came first?," we warned that it might take up to a year of careful archival work (to establish the actual dates of the facilities) and that we could not be sure that the answer would be what CBE expected—that siting dominated move-in. CBE organizers assured us that regardless of what we found, they would be able to organize about the relevant policy concerns. And this is a crucial point:

researchers are not advocates and cannot tailor their results to advocacy, and establishing relationships with community groups that understand this is important.

Even as we began work on the "which came first?" project, we also turned our attention to providing research that would back up the campaign to overturn Rule 1402, the aforementioned regulation that had elevated the level of permissible cancer risk from the emission of toxic chemicals at particular facilities. We specifically began to map the Southern California facilities listed in the U.S. Environmental Protection Agency's Toxic Release Inventory (TRI) reporting air emissions, demonstrating that these were, much like the facilities that processed hazardous waste, disproportionately concentrated in minority communities, even after controlling for other factors that might explain facility location.[20] We specifically concentrated on air release emissions of carcinogenic chemicals, the focal point of CBE organizing, and demonstrated that the degree of minority overexposure was actually more severe if one looked at just these more dangerous releases.

During this period, the two original research leads, Manuel Pastor and Jim Sadd, officially added Rachel Morello-Frosch as a full partner. Pastor, an economist and statistician, and Sadd, an expert in geographic information systems (GISs), welcomed the addition of Morello-Frosch, an environmental health scientist and epidemiologist who had produced pioneering work in the environmental justice field. Morello-Frosch brought to the collaborative her extensive analysis of the EPA's Cumulative Exposure Project and National Air Toxics Assessment data sets. Her work included conducting a tract-by-tract estimate of lifetime cancer risk associated with ambient air toxics from both mobile (cars, trucks, etc.) and stationary (industrial facilities, auto repair shops, etc.) sources.[21] With this and the TRI data, we were able to make the case that CBE had needed to press its argument for a revision of Rule 1402.

We released the results of our preliminary analysis in an opinion piece jointly authored with CBE's then Southern California director, Carlos Porras, and published in the *Los Angeles Times* on the eve of the air board's reconsideration of Rule 1402. We like to think that this had an impact on the outcome—and it likely did, particularly in terms of "legitimating" community perspectives, always an important role for researchers. Perhaps more important, however, this analysis was accompanied by the mobilization of nearly five hundred residents to attend the air board's hearings and voice their concerns. In March 2000, the air board reduced the cancer-risk threshold by 75 percent and promised to incorporate cumulative impacts into its permitting procedures as soon as feasible.

The mobilization at the air board meeting itself was an outgrowth of a patient process that included the development of an Environmental Justice Training Institute in 1999 that was coordinated by Liberty Hill. The institute provided training to smaller organizations in the fundamental aspects of organizing for environmental justice; the basics of environmental law, toxic pollutants, regulatory responsibilities, and public health standards; the use of computer research tools to generate usable maps of neighborhood issues; and the basics of maintaining a community-based organization, including grassroots fund-raising, media outreach, and working with volunteers. Aside from training, the institute helped build a base and set of regional contacts for the CBE organizing effort, and the researchers participated with presentations and bilingual training in the use of computer mapping.

The Rule 1402 victory was certainly a high point in the collaboration: research, organizing, and the facilitation role provided by a skilled philanthropic partner had come together to make real change. But there were and have been other victories along the way. At the request of CBE, the researchers performed an analysis of the expansion of the Los Angeles airport that demonstrated that the plan favored by the airport authorities and the regional planning agency was the least equitable in terms of disproportionate exposure.[22] This led the airport authority to bring on new consultants and to revise its environmental impact report to more substantively address issues of environmental justice. The researchers also began to move in the direction of the disproportionate impact of air pollution on minority schoolchildren, an effort that fit into CBE's related effort to close a chrome-plating factory operating near a school and to force the local school district to clean up toxics in a schoolyard.[23] In terms of both research and policy change, it was a very fruitful partnership.

Moving North: Reproducing the Collaborative in the San Francisco Bay Area

Even as the research–activist collaboration took firm root in Southern California, there was growing interest in whether it might have a place in the social ecology of the San Francisco Bay Area as well. After several years of thinking, planning, and requesting external support, a parallel effort was launched in 2004 that focused on the five main counties of the Bay Area.

The Bay Area is, in some ways, a more difficult place than Los Angeles for such activity. This may seem surprising, given that the Bay Area is generally thought of as more progressive in both its activist community and its institutions of higher learning and research—surely this sort of coupling of research, organizing, and policy change could easily find a home in this region. Yet the density of the Bay Area activist community can also work against the model developed in Los Angeles—existing networks mean one needs to step lightly; the process of getting to know the partners and develop trust is critical and sometimes more time-consuming.

In L.A., by contrast, pressing environmental justice issues were being addressed by a less cohesive and more locally focused environmental justice community. The early efforts of Mothers of East L.A.[24] were geographically confined to a specific local ethnic community. Concerned Citizens of South Central, which successfully resisted a municipal incinerator in its environs even after the land had been taken by eminent domain and bonds sold for the project, had gone on to work on housing issues. The Labor/Community Strategy Center, which had originally focused on air pollution issues in Wilmington, had decided to branch out in the direction of transportation justice through the development of the Bus Riders Union and its successful challenge to the regional transportation agency.[25] Therefore, in Southern California, CBE had been able to play the primary role of stitching together smaller community-based groups on a political landscape less crowded by already existing and competing groups.[26]

The Bay Area is, as noted, thicker in both existing organizations and political histories. Thus, the replication model for Northern California has involved less a sort of standalone tripartite model—a philanthropic organization, CBE, and the research team—and more a coalitional effort. In this case, the local philanthropic partner is the San Francisco Foundation—the largest community foundation in the country and one that has a proud progressive tradition but is less firmly identified with the activist community than Liberty Hill. And in this collaboration, again funded by the California Endowment, the three partners are anchors but the project has brought together other coalitions of existing environmental justice organizations to work together on a shared project around cumulative exposure to air pollution.

Given that the Bay Area collaborative is still in its infancy, there is less to report in terms of concrete results. Important process lessons are already clear, however. These include the need to go slow, to respect community voice in terms of deciding which environmental justice issues are critical, and to be clear about the respective roles of researchers and community activists. Although in its infancy, the move northward—particularly given the anticipatory planning period and discussions between 2002 and 2004—has had an important impact on our research. From scholars primarily concerned with exposures in Southern California, we have developed a statewide agenda, beginning with a series of statewide analyses of air quality.[27] This statewide focus arose partly because we were preparing for covering the Bay Area but also because of the style of community engagement that had evolved in our work. In particular, several environmental justice groups with whom we were working in different ways (including CBE in Los Angeles, Urban Habitat in the Bay Area, and the Environmental Health Coalition in San Diego) wished to take advantage of a changing policy environment at the state level. As it turns out, the California Environmental Protection Agency (CALEPA), the umbrella agency for the state's various regulatory agencies, developed a set of comprehensive recommendations on the implementation of environmental justice mandates passed by state legislators after 1999.[28] Environmental justice groups wished to influence the evolution of these recommendations, and our statewide studies provided firmer ground for their concerns. As a result, while one might surmise that a move to the statewide policy level would attenuate our relationships with local environmental justice groups (as when researchers jump to a "higher" level to talk with "important" policymakers), this did not occur in our case. This statewide work instead grew out of, and strengthened and broadened, our work with community-based environmental justice advocates. This was partly because our research agenda was responding to their organizing agenda—and partly because while we provided background research, the activists themselves served on advisory panels and carried the recommendations forward.

Moreover, we have also cast a statewide look at the impact of air pollution on academic scores for schoolchildren.[29] The latter was an especially interesting project as it reflected just how much our own research agenda had been transformed by our continuing work with CBE and other activists.

While the project on air pollution and academic performance was entirely a research effort and funded apart from our regular collaborative, it grew out of our original work on disproportionate exposures conducted at the request of CBE. We were specifically interested in finding out whether air pollution, perhaps through increasing asthma vulnerabilities, might have an impact on the academic success (as measured by standardized test scores) of children in highly polluted areas. The short answer is that it does, even when you control for the other factors (such as family poverty and parent education) that are often associated with academic outcomes.

But the focus we wish to take here is not on the results of the research but on the process and how we have incorporated lessons learned from the CBE partnership. First, we decided to do the work in a way that would include both the Bay Area and the Los Angeles metropolitan area, thinking that this would be a useful way to effectively introduce ourselves to that latter com-munity.[30] Aside from expanding the scope of our study, we included in the plan a series of preview meetings with environmental justice and children's advocates. That is, after the research had been completed but before either a technical or popular report had been written, we wanted to understand the organizing and policy context in which the research would be delivered, and so we convened a group of around twenty organizational and community-based leaders in Los Angeles and around thirty such community leaders in Oakland to gauge the reaction.

It was an extraordinarily useful set of sessions. In Los Angeles, the focus was on the fact that our study looked at air toxics, which tend to be higher in urban areas, rather than pesticides and criteria pollutants (such as ozone and particulates), and activists stressed the notion that our conclusions should emphasize the need to consider all pollutants and create better statewide data systems. In the Bay Area, activists rightly pointed out the worry that our finding that pollution negatively affected academic perform-ance could lead to further abandonment of the inner city—suburban school districts are "safer" in terms of air pollution—and argued that we should be clear that our results were the basis for a call for cleanup and not middle-class flight. These ideas and more were incorporated, and the product was better as a result.

That we conducted such meetings with community leaders before we had even previewed the results to other academics or to policymakers reflects, as we have noted, an important change in the way we now do our work. We have found that interaction with community groups does not diminish the scientific content of the work even as it elevates the practical appeal and likelihood that the results will have "policy legs." In short, much as our work may have helped transform the landscape of environmental justice organiz-ing and policy in California, it has had an important impact on transforming us as researchers and activists.

Looking Back, Looking Forward:
Reflections on the Work and the Process

When outsiders think of the relationship between academic researchers and community groups, the image that sometimes arises is one of tensions about cross-purposes and varying class and professional backgrounds. The chapters in this volume offer a different view, but the risks of bad collaborations—which then spoil the ground for other partners—should be discussed explic-itly, in order to understand how things can be different.

Many academics are familiar with the litany of issues that community organizers and community residents suggest characterize flawed collaborations. These include a tendency of academics to forget about underlying differences in power, prestige, and security; to create an excessive strain on shared financial resources because of the high costs of supporting university-based research; to unilaterally define the research topics and methodology without significant dialogue with community partners; and to focus on creating information-rich reports and academic publications while failing to generate and process continuing research at the community level.[31]

We have been fortunate to be able to avoid several (but not all) of these pitfalls in our work. We have been conscious of power differences, generally taken the lowest share of financial resources in collaborations and sometimes returned unused funds for use by the collaborative, shared research decision processes if not always the research itself, and worked, particularly in collaboration with Liberty Hill's Environmental Justice Institute discussed earlier, to help expand community capacity. But collaboration means trust and power-sharing and, in this light, it is important to note that while the usual criticisms of partnerships usually come from the community side, these issues and tensions can cut both ways. As humble as we think academics should be—we can't move policy through good science in the absence of community organizing partners—researchers also have needs that must be met in the collaboration. Academics, in short, should not act superior—but they also need not simply be subservient.

In striking the balance, it is important to maintain mutual respect for differing skills and predilections. Academics sometimes fail to understand just how challenging community organizing can be and assume that all the tough work happens in research and number crunching. At the same time, sometimes communities demand "authenticity"—a demonstration that one is truly "with the neighborhood" in its struggle. Some academics try to meet this demand by trying to transform themselves into organizers who attend every meeting and protest but forgetting that community members are the real experts at grassroots mobilization. Therefore, it seems to us that it would be a better use of our time to run complicated regressions than to try to replicate what our community partners can accomplish more effectively than us.

A second key element that we think makes for good partnerships is a true respect for the rigor and objectivity of science. We have been blessed to collaborate with community organizations that understand that while they exercise strong influence over the choice of research topics, the results will be dictated by the data. This is a key difference with some variants of action research—which often involves marshalling evidence in support of an argument one already believes to be true (such as demonstrating that increasing the minimum wage is "good") or finding specific information about an opponent on the other side of a debate (say, a company that wants to site a hazardous facility). Academics generally do not address questions where they know the answer in advance—and engaging an analysis to "demonstrate" that environmental racism exists is fundamentally different than testing the hypothesis that it does.

A third issue is understanding the rather limited support in the university for progressive academics who undertake community-based collaborations. While this set of co-authors has been fortunate to be in generally supportive settings, not every academic is so lucky. Often, adventurous academics who are themselves resentful of academic conservatism will nevertheless face community resentment of their university's activities or the academy in general. Moreover, community allies may not realize how isolated and precarious a researcher's position might be at his or her own institution. Of course, this also places an onus on researchers to transform academic structures in order to overcome this isolation. Researchers can achieve this by linking up with and vigorously supporting like-minded colleagues, especially junior colleagues and graduate students, to define a new model of engaged scholarship that can stand up to scrutiny in a university setting and successfully secure one of the primary rewards guaranteeing academic freedom: tenure and promotion. The issues related to this long and difficult process must, at a minimum, be explained to community partners to help them understand the challenges faced by their academic allies.

While there are likely more issues that should be communicated to community partners regarding successful collaboration, given the audience for this volume, we focus now on what we think might be generally important lessons from our work for other professionals working at the intersection of institutions, communities, and social justice movements.

First, while academic collaborators can play a useful role on certain specific policy questions, one of the most significant contributions is helping to create *a frame for change*. While we have engaged in several specific projects, such as the aforementioned analysis of the expansion of the Los Angeles airport, we have generally focused our attention on assessing how environmental disparities play out in California. We have contributed to a wave of studies that have successfully countered the critics of environmental justice, and the organizations with which we have worked are now actively negotiating approaches to cumulative exposure or the precautionary principle with key agencies rather than establishing that they need to be listened to in the first place.[32] In short, policymakers are now less focused on *whether* there is a problem and are turning their attention to *what to do about it*—and this is exactly the shift in consciousness that our community allies were hoping to achieve through their work and their research relationship with us.

A research focus on assessing and making the case for broad environmental disparity may seem like an odd choice, particularly given the immediacy of many of the health issues threatening low-income communities in Southern California and elsewhere in this country. Yet many progressive community leaders and organizers have taken to heart the success of the conservative movement in shaping the ideas that inform debates, policies, and votes. Demonstrating that there is a "commonality of disparity" and changing the media frame and popular sentiment around the problem is crucial.[33] It allows for a platform for specific actions such as changes in air quality rules, the adoption of cumulative exposure strategies by the state, and the push for cleaner, safer schools—in short, it is the investment in the big case for change that often helps set and reinforce the stage for community victories.[34]

A second lesson is the need to *build organic relationships between partners*. One unique feature of our original Southern California collaboration is that it was forged out of mutual interest and trust in one another, and not out of financial opportunity. With community–university partnerships now a foundation and government fad, requests for proposals will inevitably lead to collaborations that will be based on short-term intersections rather than long-term alliances. The latter are more sustainable, even when cash is short, and it suggests that researchers and communities should move as slowly as needed to build the necessary trust. In our expansion to Northern California, for example, we have worked slowly, selectively, and carefully to expand our circles.

Of course, sometimes time is short and opportunities or challenges are pressing. In both these cases and in longer-term collaborations, Swati Prakash, former environmental health director for the Harlem-based WE ACT for Environmental Justice, suggests that written documents may be useful for establishing parameters and understandings.[35] Our own decision-making process for selecting research projects was developed through a memorandum of understanding after some crossed signals over a particular effort led to a collective desire by all partners to clarify our implicit agreements. Still, there needs to be a foundation of trust based on repeated interactions, so when moments of frustration or doubt arise, there is a commitment to stick with the partnership and learn from any mistakes for the next time of challenge.[36]

A third lesson is the need to *communicate results simply without oversimplification*. There is sometimes a tendency, by either researchers or policymakers, to underappreciate community intellect and scientific literacy. But anyone working with community organizations (and certainly that includes the authors in this volume) will testify to the savvy of community leaders and their ability to process and leverage scientific and statistical information. In our work, we find that we have sometimes been told by foundations and other professionals that we should tone down the work and simplify our PowerPoints; we find that community leaders, on the other hand, want as much sophistication as we can muster so that they can more effectively engage in "data judo" with regulators and policymakers.[37]

At the same time, it is important to have a well-developed communication strategy to get the results out to the public. We have generally tried to ensure that every academic paper has a corresponding opinion piece, and we have published such pieces in the *Los Angeles Times*, the *San Jose Mercury News*, and elsewhere, often timing the articles to affect upcoming decisions by regulators where CBE and other allies are organizing for impact. We have participated in "toxic tours" arranged by CBE—these involve taking key policymakers, funders, and others on a trek through polluted areas to see the concrete conditions residents face as well as hear their stories, often after we have first established the general picture through a research overview. And we have copublished with our partners in both scientific journals[38] and the popular press.

A fourth lesson is to *understand the limited role of research in social change*. There is a tendency, particularly given the training in the academy, to think that a good argument and a well-supported set of facts will move policy. But if this were so, we would not be treated to the current specter of school boards trying to insert religious curriculum in science classes or economic policymakers insisting that cutting taxes will shrink government deficits. At the heart of change is power, and being invited to play an "inside game" of testimony to policymakers will not shift minds if community organizers are not alongside to mobilize the numbers that signal the political and social costs to evading community concerns.

This is not to dismiss research—or the commitment to objectivity we have insisted on above—but rather to acknowledge, as do Renée, Oakes, Rogers, and Blasi in their contribution to this volume, that "technical knowledge is only one part of the larger struggle." Partly because of that, and because of our own commitment to social change, we have worked with our partners to see that the benefits of funds raised for our efforts go for mobilizing communities to participate in public action and debate. Investments in experts like ourselves are, of course, a necessary part of the effort, but investments in organizing and building capacity at the community level are essential.

A fifth lesson is that *collaboration improves the quality of the research*. The usual thought about collaborations focuses on the ways that research enhances community groups' effectiveness. In Southern California, for example, CBE worked directly with researchers to provide organizers access to maps and statistical analyses that improved their credibility when presenting arguments in working groups, policy meetings, and other settings. CBE also used some of our techniques and data as a template for their own analyses. Yet it is equally true that the quality of our academic work and the sophistication of our methods were enriched as a result of the collaboration.

On the one hand, our community partners often have an organic sense of what topics are important—both what might be most responsive to community concerns but also what is relevant to advancing the general framework of environmental justice. Many of our "best" ideas have emerged from comment or insight by a community member—exploring the disparities faced by schoolchildren, for example, rose out of the concerns of our allies. Our policy recommendations have benefited, as in the aforementioned discussion of children's health and schools, from community organizers who know the policymaking terrains and the ways findings can be misinterpreted. Moreover, and just as important, our relationships with communities have led us as researchers to be even more careful about techniques and statistical strategies. After all, the results will have to face multiple tests, including academic reviews, policy presentations, and, not least, community wisdom. And because the results may actually be used to move policy and not just create additions to our resumes, we have wanted to make sure we have conducted our work as carefully, soberly, and intelligibly as possible.

The result, happily enough for us, has been a solid stream of academic publications, foundation funding, and engagement with policymakers. Our experience offers a simple lesson for students, professors, and researchers embarking (or continuing) on this sort of academic path: "engaged scholarship" is an effective, innovative research strategy that can be enriching in unpredictable ways.

Nevertheless, conducting engaged scholarship has some critical challenges that researchers should be aware of. First, much of this work requires interdisciplinary collaboration. Our research team encompasses training in the fields of economics, environmental health science, epidemiology, geographical information systems, and statistics. This means that our publication strategy entails disseminating our work to a broad academic audience through peer-reviewed publications in journals representing diverse disciplines. Although these types of research partnerships are intellectually challenging and stimulating, some academic institutions may have difficulty evaluating the work of such an interdisciplinary research venture. Moreover, securing funding from traditional federal sources, such as the National Science Foundation and the National Institutes of Health, may require persistent and innovative grantsmanship strategies. This situation may pose unique challenges for junior scholars whose research and fund-raising capacity generally form the basis for their promotion and tenure reviews. Nevertheless, within those academic institutions that promote interdisciplinary work, this type of engaged and collaborative scholarship may be strongly supported, and ultimately it is a style of work (living collaborations connected to real social actors and the capacity to see ideas transform into concrete policy action) that is motivating, satisfying, and inspiring.

Many academic–community collaboratives also require significant staffing resources. Yet, finding appropriate people to hire can be a challenge, especially when it's critical to find students or staff members who can successfully engage with community members individually and to work in collective situations where collaborative decisions are being made and strategies for research or advocacy are being debated. Indeed, building successful and sustainable academic–community collaboratives takes time and commitment, and this can be frustrating for those academics who may be used to independently launching their research, writing their grants, and cranking out publications. In order to earn the trust and respect of community partners, professionals must expect to spend a significant amount of time getting to know colleagues through meaningful interactions that transcend a traditional research role. This may entail developing, leading, and participating in trainings and the "power analysis" usually conducted before campaigns, helping to build capacity of community-based organizations through specific assistance, developing and disseminating accessible materials that community members can use in their own work, and sitting on boards of directors and showing up for community events that are components of the collaborative's advocacy and organizing goals.

Finally, although one develops deep personal connections with individuals within a community–academic collaborative, the sustainable relationships forged are fundamentally institutional. Keeping this dynamic in mind helps collaborative members deal with personnel and staffing changes that inevitably happen within partnering organizations. This occurred within our collaborative with CBE, when the organization hired a new executive director. The strong institutional alliances forged between the participating organizations enabled the Southern California collaboration to successfully weather this significant leadership transition.

Despite its inherent challenges, the field of "engaged scholarship" linking research to social justice advocacy and community-based activism is thriving.

Many researchers in both the sciences and social sciences have come to real-ize that such engaged scholarship helps them become powerful agents for pol-icy change without compromising the standards of rigorous scientific research. Indeed, academic–community research collaboratives promote not only good science but science that is focused on critical problems that affect the lives of real people, while also enhancing community capacity and participation in re-search and advocacy. In terms of promoting principles of environmental jus-tice in both the academic and policy arenas, building community–academic collaboratives through engaged scholarship can be an excellent strategy for broadening constituencies and helping to develop a new generation of en-gaged professionals committed to the public understanding of the connections between social justice, racial equality, public health, and environmental sus-tainability.

Notes

1. Ken Geiser and Gerry Waneck, "PCBs and Warren County," in *Unequal Pro-tection: Environmental Justice and Communities of Color*, ed. Robert D. Bullard (San Francisco: Sierra Club Books, 1994), 43–52.

2. U.S. General Accounting Office, *Siting of Hazardous Waste Landfills and Their Correlation with Racial and Economic Status of Surrounding Communities* (Gaithersburg, MD: U.S. General Accounting Office, 1983).

3. United Church of Christ, *A National Report on the Racial and Socio-economic Characteristics of Communities with Hazardous Waste Sites* (New York: United Church of Christ, Commission for Racial Justice, 1987).

4. Robert D. Bullard, *Dumping in Dixie: Race, Class, and Environmental Quality* (Boulder, CO: Westview Press, 1990).

5. See James P. Lester, David W. Allen, and Kelly M. Hill, *Environmental Justice in the United States: Myths and Realities* (Boulder, CO: Westview Press, 2001); and Bunyan Bryant and Paul Mohai, eds., *Race and the Incidence of Environmental Haz-ards* (Boulder, CO: Westview Press, 1992). Legal professionals have also played an important role in the environmental justice movement, and much of the research even has been published in law journals; see, for example, Vicki Been, "Analyzing Evidence of Environmental Justice," *Journal of Land Use and Environmental Law* 11 (Fall 1995): 1–37; and Vicki Been and Francis Gupta, "Coming to the Nuisance or Going to the Barrios? A Longitudinal Analysis of Environmental Justice Claims," *Ecology Law Quarterly* 24 (1997): 1–56. For one important account of legal and com-munity struggles in rural communities in California—and the evolving balance of organizing and litigation as well as the transformation of the lawyers themselves—see Luke W. Cole and Shelia R. Foster, *From the Ground Up: Environmental Racism and the Rise of the Environmental Justice Movement* (New York: New York University Press, 2001).

6. One exception was an environmental justice analysis of the expansion of the Los Angeles International Airport, conducted at the request of community partners seeking to slow or stop airport expansion. The analysis, which was released as a report and then led to an opinion piece in the *Los Angeles Times* and coverage in the *Wall Street Journal*, raised enough concerns to trigger a deeper environmental impact report (see Manuel Pastor and James Sadd, "Put LAX Expansion in a Holding Pattern Pending Further Research," *Los Angeles Times*, November 15, 2000, B13, and the discussion later in the text). The airport authorities agreed to a Community Benefits Agreement that included significant environmental remediation for nearby minority communities (see www.laane.org).

7. Douglas Anderton, Andy Anderson, Peter Rossi, John Oakes, Michael Fraser, Eleanor Weber, and Edward Calabrese, "Hazardous Waste Facilities: Environmental Equity Issues in Metropolitan Areas," *Evaluation Review* 18 (1994): 123–40; Christopher Foreman, *The Promise and Peril of Environmental Justice* (Washington, DC: Brookings Institution, 1998); and W. Bowen, *Environmental Justice through Research-Based Decision-making* (New York: Garland Publishing, 2001).

8. United Church of Christ, *National Report*.

9. Anderton et al., "Hazardous Waste"; and Douglas Anderton, Andy Anderson, John Oakes, and Michael Fraser, "Environmental Equity: The Demographics of Dumping," *Demography* 31 (1994): 229–48.

10. See Anderton et al., "Hazardous Waste"; Anderton et al., "Environmental Equity"; and Paul Mohai and Robin Saha, "Reassessing Race and Socioeconomic Disparities in Environmental Justice Research," *Demography* 43, no. 2 (2006).

11. Vicki Been, "Analyzing Evidence"; and Evan J. Ringquist, "Assessing the Evidence Regarding Environmental Inequities: A Meta-Analysis," *Journal of Policy Analysis and Management* 24, no. 2 (2005): 223–47.

12. Manuel Pastor, Robert D. Bullard, James Boyce, Alice Fothergill, Rachel Morello-Frosch, and Beverly Wright, *In the Wake of the Storm: Environment, Disaster, and Race* (New York: Russell Sage Foundation, 2006).

13. James L. Sadd, Manuel Pastor, J. Tom Boer, and Lori Snyder, "'Every Breath You Take . . .': The Demographics of Toxic Air Releases in Southern California," *Economic Development Quarterly* 13, no. 2 (May 1999): 107–23.

14. Michael Ash and T. R. Fetter, "Who Lives on the Wrong Side of the Environmental Tracks? Evidence from the EPA's Risk-Screening Environmental Indicators Model," *Social Science Quarterly* 85, no. 2 (June 2004): 441–62.

15. The transformation appears to have been significant: J. Thomas Boer, Esq., is an environmental lawyer with the U.S. Department of Justice specializing in hazardous waste regulation, and Lori Snyder Bennear, PhD, is an assistant professor of environmental economics and policy at Duke University.

16. Joel T. Boer, Manuel Pastor, James L. Sadd, and Lori D. Snyder, "Is There Environmental Racism? The Demographics of Hazardous Waste in Los Angeles County," *Social Science Quarterly* 78, no. 4 (1997): 793–810.

17. Susan Moffat, "Minorities Found More Likely to Live Near Toxic Sites," *Los Angeles Times*, August 30, 1995, B1.

18. Dara O'Rourke and Gregg P. Macey, "Community Environmental Policing: Assessing New Strategies of Public Participation in Environmental Regulation," *Journal of Policy Analysis and Management* 22, no. 3 (2003): 383–414.

19. In another example of the "triangle" strategy, in 1997, CBE became concerned that the South Coast Air Quality Management District's (SCAQMD) Rule 1610 allowed oil companies operating marine loading facilities to avoid installing vapor recovery equipment, otherwise required by regulation, and offset those emissions by scrapping older cars in the four-county air basin. While this "market-based" scheme was supposed to result in a net reduction in air pollution throughout the region, it allowed for the persistence of "hot spots" in the low-income and minority community of Wilmington. CBE confronted the SCAQMD and the State of California under Title VI of the Civil Rights Act, and while the lawsuit was working through the courts and administrative channels, CBE's organizers went door to door, distributing information and convening more than two hundred community residents at town hall–style forums with SCAQMD officials. The combination resulted in an unprecedented moratorium on pollution credit trading plans in the State of California, secured a mobile asthma clinic and agreements to use proper equipment at the port, and gave impetus, along with other pressures documented here, to the SCAQMD's eventual adoption of a ten-point "Environmental Justice Initiative."

20. Sadd et al., "Every Breath."

21. U.S. Environmental Protection Agency, *National Air Toxics Assessment (NATA): National-Scale Air Toxics Assessment* (Washington, DC: U.S. Environmental Protection Agency, 2005), available at: www.epa.gov/ttn/atw/nata/; Rachel Morello-Frosch, Tracey J. Woodruff, Daniel Axelrad, and Jane Caldwell, "Air Toxics and Health Risks in California: The Public Health Implications of Outdoor Concentrations," *Risk Analysis* 20, no. 2 (2000): 273–91; and Rachel Morello-Frosch, Manuel Pastor, and James L. Sadd, "Environmental Justice and Southern California's 'Riskscape': The Distribution of Air Toxics Exposures and Health Risks Among Diverse Communities," *Urban Affairs Review* 36, no. 4 (March 2001): 551–78.

22. Sadd et al., "Every Breath."

23. Jose Cardenas, "School's Tainted Soil to Be Removed," *Los Angeles Times*, May 31, 2001.

24. The early efforts of Mothers of East L.A. is well documented in Gabriel Gutiérrez, "Mothers of East Los Angeles Strike Back," in *Unequal Protection: Environmental Justice and Communities of Color*, ed. Robert. D. Bullard (San Francisco: Sierra Club Books, 1994).

25. Eric Mann, *A New Vision for Urban Transportation: The Bus Riders Union Makes History at the Intersection of Mass Transit, Civil Rights, and the Environment* (Los Angeles: Labor/Community Strategy Center, 1996); and Manuel Pastor, "Common Ground at Ground Zero? The New Economy and the New Organizing in Los Angeles," *Antipode* 33, no. 2 (March 2001): 260–89.

26. Other groups have been able to do this as well, including the Center for the Law in the Public Interest, which has stressed open parks and green space as part of an environmental justice agenda for low-income communities of color in Southern California. And the networks in Southern California have certainly thickened in intervening years, something which has led CBE to be more of an "important among many" organization. Still, at the time CBE was starting its Los Angeles efforts, there were fewer large groups and hence many openings for this sort of broad, regionwide organizing.

27. Manuel Pastor, James Sadd, and Rachel Morello-Frosch, "Waiting to Inhale: The Demographics of Toxic Air Releases in 21st Century California," *Social Science Quarterly* 85, no. 2 (2004): 420–40; and Manuel Pastor, James Sadd, and Rachel Morello-Frosch, "The Air Is Always Cleaner on the Other Side: Race, Space, and Air Toxics Exposures in California," *Journal of Urban Affairs* 27, no. 2 (2005): 127–48.

28. See Liberty Hill Foundation, *Building a Regional Voice for Environmental Justice* (Santa Monica, CA: Liberty Hill, 2004); and Martha Matsuoka, ed., *Building Healthy Communities from the Ground Up: Environmental Justice in California* (September 2003), available at: www.calendow.org/reference/publications/pdf/disparities/TCE0915-2003_Building_Heath.pdf.

29. Manuel Pastor, Rachel Morello-Frosch, and James Sadd, *Reading, Writing, and Breathing: Schools, Air Toxics, and Environmental Justice in California* (Santa Cruz, CA: Center for Justice, Tolerance, and Community, UC Santa Cruz, 2005).

30. We should note that we were not entirely new to the Bay Area: Morello-Frosch had worked with a number of groups there, and Pastor has a long-standing collaboration on issues of regional equity with one of the leading environmental justice groups, Urban Habitat (see Juliet Ellis, Manuel Pastor, Rachel Rosner, and Elizabeth Tan, "Bridging the Bay," in *Building Sustainable Metropolitan Communities: Breakthrough Stories*, ed. Paloma Pavel [Cambridge, MA: MIT Press, 2006]). But this was among our first moves as a full research team into the Bay.

31. Swati Prakash, "Power, Privilege and Participation: Meeting the Challenge of Equal Research Alliances," *Race, Poverty and the Environment* (Winter 2004): 16.

32. Our work is part of a broad confirming trend in the literature. A recent national study by three researchers who were initially skeptical of environmental justice claims did find evidence of disparities by race and class, depending on the geographic scale used (see Lester et al., *Environmental Justice*). For a meta-study of other statistical studies in which the author concludes that while "(s)ome scholars have protested that race-based inequities are limited in scope, produced by misspecified models, or are artifacts of aggregation bias . . . protests claiming that these factors can explain away such inequities are empirically unsustainable," see Ringquist, op. cit., 241. Ringquist does note that the income results are mixed, but this squares with our own notion that higher probabilities of being near an environmental disamenity actually peaks somewhere in the income distribution rather than being monotonically increasing with wealth.

33. In 2002, for example, the Public Policy Institute of California asked respondents about their sense of environmental disparities in California and found that 58 percent agreed that lower-income and minority neighborhoods were likely to have more than their fair share of toxic wastes and polluting facilities compared to other neighborhoods. Strikingly, the perception difference between whites and Latinos—the two largest ethnic groups in the survey and the only ones for which breakdowns would be statistically reliable—were nearly indistinguishable (61 percent of Latinos believe that low-income and minority communities were more likely to be proximate to such environmental disamenities, versus 58 percent of non-Hispanic whites); see Mark Baldassare, *PPIC Statewide Survey: Special Survey on Californians and the Environment* (San Francisco: Public Policy Institute of California, 2002), available at www.ppic.org/content/pubs/survey/S_602MBS.pdf. Perceptions were also remarkably consistent across broad income levels.

34. At the same time, our relative inattention to action research did cause some frustrations with community groups funded by Liberty Hill that believed that they would have access to a sort of "rapid-response" research team. Managing these sorts of expectations is an important part of any collaborative process.

35. Prakash, "Power, Privilege and Participation."

36. A related point is to not ignore the need for extensive project coordination. In our case, Liberty Hill served much of this function, but one partner needs to be designated with those responsibilities.

37. Rachel Morello-Frosch, Manuel Pastor, James L. Sadd, Carlos Porras, and Michele Prichard, "Citizens, Science, and Data Judo: Leveraging Community-Based Participatory Research to Build a Regional Collaborative for Environmental Justice in Southern California," in *Methods for Conducting Community-Based Participatory Research in Public Health*, ed. Barbara Israel, Eugenia Eng, Amy Shultz, and Edith Parker (San Francisco: Jossey-Bass Press, 2005).

38. Rachel Morello-Frosch, Manuel Pastor, Carlos Porras, and James L. Sadd, "Environmental Justice and Regional Inequality in Southern California: Implications for Future Research," *Environmental Health Perspectives* 110, no. 2 (April 2002): 149–54.

~

CHAPTER FIVE

The Production of Knowledge and Community Empowerment: Organizing and Research on Youth Violence

Howard Pinderhughes

Youth violence has become one of the most persistent and troubling social problems in contemporary U.S. society. To many Americans, youth violence is a veritable epidemic, with each new incident stunning the public with the ever-increasing brutality of the crime and youthfulness of the perpetrators. Youth violence appears as a social problem just barely contained by established social norms and legal codes, and each new horrific event reported by the media reinforces public perception of youth violence—and of inner-city youth themselves—as increasingly dangerous, unpredictable, and spiraling "out of control."

Unfortunately, the sensational cases of school massacres, elementary school shootings, and children killing children tend to distort our perceptions of the dynamics of violence in the lives of youth. The public perception of these incidents obscures the reality of the ever-present violence that some youth face in their day-to-day lives and undermines our ability to understand the effects on young people of growing up in violent environments and the ways they cope with violence. From outside of communities where high rates of violence occur, an act of violence is seen as an individual crime—a morally reprehensible act except when perpetrated by law enforcement on criminals or the armed forces in the alleged defense of democracy and freedom. Within these communities violence is also understood to be embedded in institutional arrangements that produce profound social inequalities, and as the result, violence is understood as a symptom of larger structural problems.

There is no issue on the political and social landscape today that affects inner-city communities more than the problem of youth violence. Systematic inequality, structural unemployment, entrenched poverty, neighborhood economic decay, ineffective and dysfunctional schools, and high rates of juvenile incarceration have combined in a perfect storm, producing high rates of youth violence in poor communities of color across the nation. The communities most affected by violence are the same communities which suffer from a range of structural conditions that restrict educational opportunities, compromise the health of community residents, limit employment options, and deaden aspirations and hopes for many young people who must negotiate these difficult conditions and dangerous environments, that is, inner-city areas of racial segregation and concentrated poverty. Typically, the communities that are worst hit by these problems are treated as pathological places by social theorists, policymakers, and service providers, making community residents' own understanding of their problems irrelevant at best and problematic at worst.

In the face of decades of failed policies, residents of inner-city communities across the country are struggling to find ways to reverse the trends of increasing violence, to protect their young people, and to create safer, healthier communities. Typically, community-based discussions about the problems of violence are linked with efforts to address the violent effects of structural inequality on low-income, minority communities. These communities have been subject to decades of the violence of systematic racial and class oppression ranging from employment and housing discrimination to government neglect, capital disinvestment, urban renewal, and poorly funded and dysfunctional schools. Many of these communities have experienced outright violence from the criminal justice system in the form of police brutality, disproportionate arrest, and incarceration.

Given the failure of dominant policies and practices in these communities, and the urgent needs of people living in inner-city communities, there are also few issues where community involvement in research and policy development is more needed than in the area of youth violence. From a community perspective, there can be little doubt that research and policy should begin with the conditions of inequality as the unit of analysis. But, even as community-based advocates argue that youth violence is virtually mass-produced through structural conditions, social forces, and cultural messaging, the predominant research paradigms and almost all of the policy on youth violence focus on the individual level. Much of the literature across different disciplines and perspectives analyzes youth violence as a behavior of an individual which must be explained.[1] The conclusions of such an individual-level approach reinforces the popular construction of youth violence as the product of bad kids from bad families with bad values who come from bad neighborhoods.

For the past fifteen years I have been working in communities in the San Francisco Bay Area that have experienced high levels of violence since the 1990s and which have had to deal with sharp rises in youth violence over the past four years. While rates of juvenile crimes and arrests have gone down both statewide and nationally over the last five years, these communities have experienced consistently high rates of youth violent crime and homicide.[2] Over the past three years, particularly, these communities have experienced an increase in youth violence marked by numerous deaths of young people by firearm violence. As a scholar committed to addressing the problems of youth in inner-city communities of color, I have been confronted with the multiple dilemmas that community members face in their attempts to effect local, state, and federal policies that could assist their efforts to reduce the levels of violence that plague their neighborhoods.

When I entered the field fifteen years ago to begin my research on youth violence, I brought with me very traditional methodological approaches and constructions of my identity and role as an academic. I swiftly discovered that the model of the expert scholar who conducts detached, "objective" research and retreats to his or her office to analyze the results and write articles reporting the findings was somewhat contradictory to my goals of promoting positive community change and social justice. I also discovered that I was asking the wrong questions. An outsider asks the questions, "What is wrong with those kids? Why are they so violent?" The very structure of these questions focuses the lens of inquiry at the individual level. Community members, who have watched neighborhood children grow up and change, are more likely to ask, "What happened to our children that made them violent?" It's a different perspective, one that is more consistent with understanding the root causes of violence and searching for approaches to preventing violence.

Having grown up in the predominantly black Roxbury section of Boston, I had experienced much the same process, as did childhood friends of mine who became involved in violent behavior as teenagers. When I began my career as a research scientist studying youth violence, upon reflecting on my own background and history I realized that I was ignoring the potential for the research process itself to produce important outcomes. The very process of generating the research question, developing questions and measures, interviewing subjects, and coding and analyzing the data has the potential to enhance the knowledge, understanding, and expertise that community members can utilize to develop and improve prevention programs and to advocate and shape policies designed to deal with root causes and enhance resiliency factors. Best of all, I discovered that community-based research can also help community members develop the conceptual and theoretical language and the cultural capital necessary to be effective in the policy arena. As a consequence, community members, armed with research findings, are often the most effective advocates for policies that systematically address the problems of youth violence. I have evolved my methodology toward a community-based participatory research model that engages community members in every phase of the research process. The result is research that is not only informed by community knowledge and expertise but that is shaped and conducted with community members and is of direct and practical use to members seeking to alter the conditions that produce youth violence.

Fundamentally, community members have extensive knowledge, expertise, and understanding of the causes of violence. Their experiences with violence are connected to their broader experiences of structural inequalities that shape their constructions and understandings of the problem. Community members are witnesses to the violence-production process. They have a front-row seat to the development of the neighborhood's children from babies to adults. They witness the child's interactions and experiences in the schools, the initiation and incorporation into the life, customs, and patterns on the streets. They are the ultimate investigators who, while lacking the training in methods and theory, hold intimate knowledge of the process of the production of a youth who uses violence. Community members ask different questions than academic researchers precisely because they are involved, implicated, and affected.

Unfortunately, we are trained within the academy to distrust this "bias" as antithetical to valid and reliable research. In fact, research on youth violence is most often conducted with little substantive interaction with members of the community around the research questions. The community is seen as a field site to test hypotheses about the causes of youth violence. Researchers come into the community to collect data and leave to analyze their data, write up their findings, and report their results in journals far removed from the communities they have studied. This type of drive-by research often engenders bitterness and suspicion in many communities whose members fear being exploited by researchers with little benefit to the overall community. With drive-by research, the youth remain faceless and nameless, anonymous statistics, defined by their records and rap sheets with little attention to their voices, perspectives, or broader experiences. Their words, experiences, emotions, knowledge, and perspectives are most often obscured or negated within criminal justice and public health research on youth violence. In policy discussions and debates in Washington, D.C., and Sacramento, California, in numerous academic conferences convened to address the problem of youth violence, the one voice that I have noted is usually missing from the table is that of the youth themselves. The result is a reliance on existing paradigms and constructions of the problem of youth violence—racialized constructions that locate the causes of the problem of youth violence at the individual level.

Low-income, minority communities struggle to influence the public construction of the problem of violence. These communities have much at stake in terms of how violence gets defined, understood, and addressed. At every stage of the process, communities must struggle to influence research, policy, and practice approaches to the reduction and prevention of youth violence. Often, communities must struggle just to get policymakers to address the problem of violence. Over the past five years, as rates of youth violence in many inner-city communities have remained high or increased, community advocates must wait until the body count gets high enough to elevate the problem to the top of budget priorities. Then, when youth violence is acknowledged as a problem, communities must then contend with the dominant construction of the problem as a criminal justice problem. The public dialogues about inner-city youth violence are filled with analysis and images of gangbangers, "super-predators," and child murderers that fuel policy debates about the need for more cops on the street and larger juvenile jails. This is in stark contrast to public dialogues about school shootings in white, middle-class suburbs, where discussion revolves around the mental health problems of alienated suburban adolescents and the need for more psychologists and social workers.

Communities must deal not only with the effects of the violence itself but also with the ramifications and effects of societal policies to deal with the violence. The policy approach to "bad kids" is to rely on punishment and incarceration. From the broader societal perspective, the arrest and conviction of large numbers of youth from highly impacted neighborhoods is accepted as sound law enforcement strategy to promote public safety by getting criminals off the streets. From a community perspective, however, there is a great deal of ambivalence about the "get tough on crime" approach. On the one hand, community advocates usually agree that it is sometimes necessary to remove individuals who are violent and dangerous. However, current policies have failed to prevent violence for a sustained period and have instead resulted in the criminalization of large sectors of the young, inner-city male population. Estimates of the numbers of young African American males who spend time in the criminal justice system are around 30 percent.[3]

These constructions get codified in analyses and theories of the causes of youth violence that have a profound effect on community access to funding for violence prevention programs. The normal developmental path for prevention and intervention programs is that basic research identifies a set of factors that are shown to contribute to violence. Federal, state, and private funding agencies and institutions develop grant programs for projects that are designed to deal with the factors identified in the research. These steps often happen without community input or participation. At this stage community-based organizations develop programs that fit the funders' priority areas. The result is a mosaic of programs and services that don't fit together in an organized and coherent approach to improving the conditions of the community, promoting healthy children and youth, and supporting nurturing and effective families. At root, the failure of policies to curb youth violence in inner-city communities is directly linked to the problematic ways that traditional social science research on youth violence has been conducted. Research design and results, then, have real consequences in the lives of residents of low-income, minority communities. It is to a detailed examination and critique of the dominant paradigms that I now turn.

A Critique of Traditional Research Approaches to Youth Violence

The study of violence, like all research, takes place within paradigms that determine how a problem is conceptualized, operationalized, and measured. The dominant paradigms that have shaped youth violence research are criminology or the criminal justice paradigm, psychological studies of pathological behaviors, and sociological studies of deviance. The result of these ways of conceptualizing the problem is a focus on criminal or deviant behavior rather than on violence as a social relation. While violence is constructed as a criminal act by researchers, policymakers, and the police, it is often not constructed as crime by the youth who engage in it. A focus on crime leads us to view the violence through the lens of delinquency and deviance and to focus on those youth we identify as delinquent or criminal. Such an approach embraces the notion that those youth who use violence are somehow qualitatively different than youth who avoid using violence. Within these paradigms it is impossible to view violence as a "normal" and normative act that young men and women must deal with and at times resort to. The result of this perspective is punitive policies that are designed to punish and isolate the individual rather than prevention approaches that are designed to change the conditions and circumstances that mass-produce violent youth and adults.

Most studies of adolescent violence examine the attitudes, behavior, activities, and experiences of violent and/or incarcerated youth. They focus on the "perpetrators" of violence in an attempt to analyze why they engaged in violence. Researchers interested in studying youth violence recruit their subjects in juvenile justice facilities or from gangs on the street. Such an approach tends to reify the dichotomy of "violent" and "nonviolent" youth—a problematic construction that fails to adequately capture the realities of the inner city. Sociological examinations and analyses of youth violence are dominated by the criminal justice paradigm that views youth violence as a deviant behavior by young people. Analyses focus on individual motivations, individual psychology, and individual behavior. A critical examination of theories based on this paradigm will explain why I have chosen to promote the type of community-based research that gives voice to youth as the subjects and objects of violence prevention research and programs.

Theories of the Causes of Adolescent Violence

A variety of theoretical approaches to youth violence have been used to isolate the numerous factors that contribute to high levels of adolescent violence in the inner city. Epidemiological studies have revealed a number of factors which place youth "at risk" for committing or becoming victims of violence. These risk factors include poverty, single-parent female-headed families, low academic achievement, a history of child abuse, exposure to violence, head injury, impoverished neighborhoods, and violence-prone neighborhoods.[4] Studies have also shown a relationship between drug and alcohol use and violence.[5] These studies have been useful as the basis for intervention and prevention programs that have been developed at the community level. However, the link between research and program development has traditionally been quite weak. Until recently, basic research has been funded and conducted under separate funding programs than program development and evaluation.

Recently, the focus on "evidence-based" programs and practice has necessitated a closer relationship between research and practice. This focus has also increased the power of researchers to determine the parameters and foundations for prevention programs through their formulations of research questions. In this way, researchers help to set policy priorities. Unfortunately, they do so often without any input or participation from members of the effected communities.

Not all research pathologizes community youth, however. A number of studies of youth violence have clearly established that structural conditions of poverty, high exposures to violence, and poor educational and employment options place young people at higher risk of victimization and perpetration of violence.[6] Structural factors such as poverty, inequality, and limited economic opportunities have been used to explain higher rates of violence in inner-city communities.[7] Social ecological theories focus on the interaction among structural aspects of the ghetto environment to explain differential rates of violence in inner-city communities. Excessive crowding, high levels of crime and violence, social isolation from mainstream society, high levels of social disorganization, the availability of guns, social disorganization of the neighborhood, and the declining economic base of the city are all strongly related to high rates of homicide in inner-city areas.[8] High levels of family disruption are also seen as facilitating violence by decreasing community networks of social control, and neighborhoods with sparse friendship networks, unsupervised teenage peer groups, and low organizational participation have been shown to have disproportionately high levels of violence.[9] All of these structural conditions exist for the youth in inner-city communities with high levels of violence. These factors provide the necessary conditions for the high levels of violence to which the young people are exposed. This research has provided the basis for some small-scale economic development programs, employment and educational programs which seek to improve the underlying factors that help to produce violence. Unfortunately, in the policy arena the results of this research take a back seat to criminal justice and psychological research that focuses at the individual level.

Some scholars propose that the interaction of these factors fosters a subculture of violence in which aggressive behaviors, frequent interpersonal confrontations, and high risk, self-destructive activities are tolerated and positively reinforced.[10] A key aspect of early theories on the subculture of violence was the internalization of deviant values within a lower-class community.[11] Theories of the subculture of violence are particularly damaging to community efforts to prevent violence. Such theories reinforce popular images about poor African American and Latino communities and remove the focus and responsibility from the structural arrangements and the larger society. They also contribute to stereotypes about whole communities of youth when it is a minority of young people engaged in the violence. There is an undeniable cultural element to the production of violence, but it is clearly not the root cause of the violence.

Anderson describes a "code of the streets" which governs the interactions and behavior of young males in an inner-city neighborhood in

Philadelphia.[12] The code that develops among street youth and gang members becomes the dominant set of rules for engagement and interaction in the street context within a community where there are high levels of violence. One of the most important aspects of the code of the streets, Anderson shows, is that it governs the behavior of both the "street" and "decent" youth in shared public space. This happens as a result of the perception that adherence to these codes is the surest method for survival. Anderson describes the code as a cultural adaptation to the inability of the normal mechanisms of social control—such as the police, judicial system, and community social networks—to be effective. Even Anderson's attempts to raise questions about a violent subculture, however, result in a focus on the cultural production of violence rather than the production of violence as a social problem rooted in a highly structured racial system. The result is research that further demonizes both individuals and communities and does little to empower the community to address the problem of youth violence.

While such theories about deviant subcultures are consistent with dominant beliefs and constructions of the causes of youth violence, they are of limited use for community members who are seeking to prevent violence. Within these communities, and more important, among the youth themselves, the acceptance of a perceived necessity to use violence under certain situations differs from the moral condemnation of the subculture-of-violence perspective.

Recent research on violence has adopted an approach which analyzes violent events as the result of the interaction among people, their motivations, the meaning which they attribute to the interaction, and the violent act.[13] This approach takes into account the varied forces, factors, and dynamics which go into a human interaction which results in violence.[14] It does not deny the importance of individual-level factors such as character traits, SES (socioeconomic status), and so forth but argues that a violent event is not solely the result of an individual predisposition or proclivity to violence. Rather, from this perspective, cultural and situational dynamics contribute to a violent event. Violent incidents are analyzed as "situated transactions" with specific rules that develop within specific social settings.[15] In the context of the street in an inner-city neighborhood, individuals utilize "scripts" which provide a map of how to negotiate conflictual and potentially violent circumstances.[16] Fagan and Wilkinson analyze adolescent violence as a "functional, purposive behavior that serves definable goals within specific social contexts."[17] This work provides a useful foundation for understanding how violent events take place.

The youth cultural perspectives described are not deviant subcultures that embrace oppositional norms and values—rather, they are shared perceptions of the likelihood of violence in their community and of the perceived necessity to use violence under certain circumstances. These perceptions are shared by youth from many different class, race, and gender backgrounds. Contrary to theoretical approaches that analyze youth violence as a deviant subculture, this cultural youth perspective is an extension of the dominant culture that validates and legitimizes the use of power and domination particularly in the face of perceived danger. The very traits that are valorized in our nation's foreign policy—toughness, aggression, strength, and domination—are demonized when young inner-city youth display them in efforts to survive dangerous environments.

Each of these theoretical perspectives provides some insight into the larger question of the causes and consequences of youth violence. Taken together they provide the building blocks for a more comprehensive approach to understanding and dealing with youth violence. Traditional scholarly, scientific, and even policy practice does not lead us toward more comprehensive approaches to understanding and formulating policy about social problems. Theories about the causes and consequences of violence need to be more comprehensive and holistic, although they rarely are. One major problem that contributes to this fragmented approach is that standard scientific methodology calls for hypothesis testing that examines a limited number of factors as the independent variable. This restricted understanding of the scientific method often leads to a reductionist practice that tends to simplify explanations rather than complicate them. The reality is that violence is a complex problem that has multiple causes that combine in a system of production. Complex problems require complex, comprehensive solutions. Community members understand this reality and tend to ask questions that seek to examine the complex nature of the problem and are increasingly demanding comprehensive approaches to violence prevention. For this reason, community-based research on violence has the potential to produce better science, better theory, and, more important, better policy.

Through my research collaborating with youth from the communities I was studying, we have developed an analysis of youth violence as a social relation which is produced through a combination of structural, community-level and individual-level factors. The link between these different factors is the set of cultural understandings of the structural constraints and limited opportunities, the social disorganization and lack of social control at the community level, and the omnipresent danger of violence which each youth must negotiate.

Over the past year, community workers representing community-based organizations that are working on the frontlines in San Francisco communities to reduce and eliminate the violence have banded together to demand from policymakers a comprehensive plan for violence prevention. There already existed eight to ten different city initiatives, each targeting a different set of factors, all based on research findings and best practices but with little connection or collaboration across the different city initiatives.[18]

This is a classic example of the difference in approach and perspective among policymakers, researchers, and community members. Policymakers react to political pressures as a result of media coverage of the violence and politicians' eagerness to proclaim inner-city youth violence as a major problem.[19] They are usually looking for a silver bullet, the singular program or approach that will reduce violence. Community advocates have lived through the previous period of high rates of violence and the subsequent increase in city, county, and federal funding for violence prevention. As a result they have a more long-term perspective on the roots of the violence and how to develop a long-term, sustainable strategy to prevent violence through comprehensive prevention.

A Research Model for Community Empowerment

A community empowerment model for research should not only examine and analyze problems that a community faces but should develop promising approaches to address that problem. Most important, from a community perspective, is whether the research(er) contributes to a sustainable, long-term, and systematic approach to the community's problems.

To achieve these ends, a research model that is designed to promote community empowerment should seek to:

1. Investigate problems of clear relevance to communities with community involvement and leadership. An empowerment model requires the sharing of power within the research process from the very beginning of problem identification and the development of research questions.
2. Increase the legitimacy of community perspectives and voices in the policy arena. Community voices often get dismissed as biased, and their ideas and perspectives are discredited as not evidence-based. Involving community members in the research process provides a scientific foundation for their perspectives to be considered.
3. Build the sustainable capacity for communities to do research by including community members in every phase of the research process,

providing training and technical assistance, and developing a pipeline for community members to become researchers. One of the biggest problems with existing research practice is that it creates and reinforces the dependency of community members on expert academic researchers. Community members have to hope that university scholars stay engaged and involved in studying the problems of their communities.

The litmus test for empowerment research is: Does the research enhance the community's capacity to deal with the problem effectively? There are several ways that community-based participatory research can achieve community capacity building:

1. It expands the knowledge and expertise of community members who work on the problem. This facilitates the future ability of community members to engage in both research and advocacy.
2. It provides legitimacy to community perspectives and knowledge at the policy level. Within the youth violence field the legitimization of youth voices and perspectives in the policy arena is particularly important.
3. It provides a voice for community knowledge and perspectives. The research process should incorporate the ideas, perspectives, and analysis of community members. Too often, community lay knowledge is ignored in the name of scientific, "unbiased" process.
4. It places community members in a more powerful position at the local, state, or federal policy levels. For positive social change to result from any research it must have an effect on the formation of policy. A sustainable change in policy orientation would result from helping to secure a place at the policy table for community advocates and activists.

Community-Based Participatory Action Research
One model for effective collaboration of researchers with community members is community-based participatory action research (CBPR), which makes community members full partners in every phase of the research process. The value of community-based participatory action research is that the researcher working with the community can incorporate research questions about factors that are relevant from a community perspective.[20] The questions that are generated from a "scientific" perspective without consultation with community members rely on theoretical paradigms that in essence objectify the members of the community. Youth violence is a primary example of this

problem. CBPR is designed to change the relationship between the academic researcher and the community. Instead of being the object of study, community members are participants in the generation of research questions and analysis. This type of participation shifts the power dynamics of the research and provides community members with an equal position in determining the direction of the research. Community-based participatory action research is guided by the premise that research can be scholarly, rigorous science and also be intentionally designed to promote community empowerment and change. The intention is not only to contribute to the literature within the discipline but to produce research that can effect social change. It raises a question about the use of knowledge and the product of the research.

While it is important to collaborate with community members as equal partners, it is critical that the researcher not abdicate his or her role as an educated and experienced researcher. Each side comes to the research relationship with a set of assets and skills. Community members have an intimate knowledge of the problem and a perspective that is forged through experiential understanding of the problem and the dynamics of the problem. The researcher brings methodological expertise, knowledge of existing theories about the causes of youth violence, as well as professional credibility and positioning with policymakers. However, these attributes are not always assets: there are times when each of these positions can result in blinders or will be the foundation for assumptions that may not be useful or accurate. It is vital that a critical and reflexive perspective be maintained about the strengths and limitations of both professional and lay participants in the research process.

The specific goal of CBPR on youth violence is to build the community's capacity to (1) generate more applicable knowledge about the nature of violence in particular communities; (2) develop a multilayered analysis of the dynamics of the problem; (3) develop sustainable and systematic strategies to decrease youth violence within the community; (4) improve the abilities of community members as policy advocates at the local, state, and federal levels; and (5) provide legitimacy and power to community members as experts in the policy arena (a place at the table).

For example, in developing my research agenda on youth violence in San Francisco, I first made myself available as a resource to community organizations doing work on violence. When I was able to secure funding to conduct violence research, I convened a group of community members to ask what kind of research on violence they would find most useful. I outlined some of my ideas for research, and they shared theirs. Slowly and collaboratively, we developed a research agenda with several research questions. The next step was to hire research assistants from the communities that were the subject of the research. These assistants then became full partners in the research process, working with me to further develop the methodology and to carry out data collection, coding, and analysis. Not incidentally, of eight research assistants who worked on the project, two went on to earn their PhDs and are working as professors/researchers in the same community on issues of violence, and two are getting their doctoral degrees in related disciplines. We have made our data, information, and training available to a number of community members to assist their efforts to gain the attention of local and state policymakers, achieve policy change, and secure funding for local violence prevention programs.

Violence is a social problem produced by structural inequities in resources and power. It is critical to develop and utilize a research methodology that challenges rather than reinforces existing arrangements of power. By incorporating the voices, perspectives, ideas, and analysis of young people in research and policy debates about youth violence, researchers can affect how young people are perceived. It contributes to theories about youth violence by providing an alternative construction of the problem—one informed by insights forged from an insider's knowledge and perspective. It challenges that dominant construction of violence as deviance and forces a new set of theoretical questions. It also produces different data resulting from the different questions raised by young people with a unique understanding of the problem and the different analyses that results from a radically different vantage point for coding the data.

Community-based participatory research on violence has the potential to produce new and important knowledge because it incorporates questions generated from a community perspective. If the methods and research procedures are rigorous, the result is better science that expands our understanding of the problem of violence. It has the potential to inform improved policy by concentrating on a more comprehensive approach to the problem and by engaging community members in the design and implementation of prevention strategies. One of the contributing factors to the prevalence of violence in inner-city communities involves the poorly developed social networks and social support systems of inner-city youth. Community-based participatory research helps to build the capacity of community social networks and social supports and enhances the power of community members and groups as agents for social change in the policy arena.

As an alternative to this approach, I seek to promote the type of community-based research that gives voice to youth as the subjects and objects of violence prevention research and programs. A community-based research response leads us to study all the youth, including those who avoid violence as a way to understand solutions to the problem and how to prevent violence. Through developing a sample of inner-city youth who represent a range of academic achievement, race, ethnicity, and gender—and who have a range of experiences with violence—it is possible to have a more accurate picture of the urban reality, one in which the majority of inner-city young people have to deal with issues of violence almost daily and engage in physical fighting at some point.

Notes

1. Ruth E. Dennis, "Social Stress and Mortality among Nonwhite Males," *Phylon* 38 (1977): 315–28 (1977), and "Homicide among Black Males: Social Costs to Families and Communities," *Public Health Reports* 95 (1980): 556–57; John Dollard, Neal E. Miller, Leonard W. Doob, O. Hobart Mowrer, and Robert R. Sears, *Frustration and Aggression* (New Haven, CT: Yale University Press, 1939); Leonard D. Eron, "Understanding Aggression," presidential address to the World Meeting of ISRA, June 12, 1990, Banff, Alberta; David P. Farrington, "Childhood Aggression and Adult Violence: Early Precursors and Later-Life Outcomes," in *The Development and Treatment of Childhood Aggression*, ed. Debra J. Pepler, Kenneth H. Rubin, et al. (Hillsdale, NJ: Lawrence Erlbaum Associates, 1991), 5–29; J. Reiss Jr. and Jeffrey A. Roth, ed., *Understanding and Preventing Violence* (Washington, DC: National Academy Press, 1993); Ingrid Waldron and Joseph Eyer, "Socioeconomic Causes of the Recent Rise in Death Rates for 15-24 Year Olds," *Social Science and Medicine* 9 (1975): 383–96.

2. Center on Juvenile and Criminal Justice, *California Youth Crime Declines: The Untold Story* (San Francisco: self-published, 2006).

3. Andrew L. Barlow, "Globalization, Racism and the Expansion of the American Penal System," in *African Americans in the U.S. Economy*, ed. Cecilia A. Conrad, John Whitehead, Patrick Mason, and James Stewart (Lanham, MD: Rowman & Littlefield, 2005), 190–201.

4. Stephen Buka and Felton Earls, "Early Determinants of Delinquency and Violence," *Health Affairs* 12 (1993): 46–64; Ronald Edari and Patricia McManus, "Risk and Resiliency Factors for Violence," *Violence Among Children and Adolescents, Pediatric Clinics of North America* 45 (1998): 293–305; Reiss and Roth, *Understanding and Preventing Violence*; Deborah Prothrow-Stith, *Deadly Consequences: How Violence Is Destroying Our Teenage Population and a Plan to Begin Solving the Problem* (New York: HarperCollins, 1991).

5. Jim Collins, "Alcohol and Interpersonal Violence: Less Than Meets the Eye," in *Pathways to Criminal Violence*, ed. Neal Alan Weiner and Marvin E. Wolfgang (Newbury Park, CA: Sage Publications, 1989), 49–67; Paul J. Goldstein, Henry H. Brownstein, Patrick Ryan, and Patricia A. Bellucci, "Crack and Homicide in New York City, 1988: A Conceptually-Based Event Analysis," *Contemporary Drug Problems* 16 (1989): 651–87.

6. Michael Green, "Youth Violence in the City: The Role of Educational Interventions," *Health Education and Behavior* 25 (1998): 175–93; Reiss and Roth, *Understanding and Preventing Violence*; Prothrow-Stith, *Deadly Consequences*; Laura Rachuba, Bonita Stanton, and Donna Howard, "Violent Crime in the United States: An Epidemiologic Profile," *Archives of Pediatrics and Adolescent Medicine* 149 (1995): 953–60; Robert J. Sampson and W. Byron Groves, "Community Structure and Crime: Testing Social-Disorganization Theory," *American Journal of Sociology* 94 (1989): 774–802.

7. James W. Balkwell, "Ethnic Inequality and the Rate of Homicide," *Social Forces* 69 (1990): 53–70; Judith R. Blau and Peter M. Blau, "The Cost of Inequality: Metropolitan Structure and Violent Crime," *American Sociological Review* 47 (1982): 114–29; Sheldon Danziger and D. Wheeler, "The Economics of Crime: Punishment or Redistribution," *Review of Social Economy* 33 (1975): 113–31; Steven F. Messner, "Poverty, Inequality, and the Urban Homicide Rate," *Criminology* (1982) 20: 103–14; Steven F. Messner, "Regional and Racial Effects on the Urban Homicide Rate: The Subculture of Violence Revisited," *American Journal of Sociology* 88 (1983): 997–1007; Steven F. Messner, "Economic Discrimination and Societal Homicide Rates: Further Evidence on the Cost of Inequality," *American Sociological Review* 54 (1989): 597–611.

8. James M. Byrne and Robert J. Sampson, "Key Issues in the Social Ecology of Crime," in *The Social Ecology of Crime*, ed. James M. Byrne and Robert J. Sampson (New York: Springer-Verlag, 1986), 1–22; Reynolds Farley, "Homicide Trends in the United States," *Demography* 17 (1980): 177–88; David P. Farrington, "Longitudinal Analysis of Criminal Violence," in *Criminal Violence*, ed. Marvin E. Wolfgang and Neal Alan Weiner (Beverly Hills, CA: Sage Publications, 1986); James F. Short Jr., "The Level of Explanation Problem in Criminology," in *Juvenile Delinquency and Urban Areas*, ed. Clifford R. Shaw and Henry D. McKay (Chicago: University of Chicago Press [1942] 1985), 51–74; Ralph Taylor and Jeanette Covington, "Neighborhood Changes in Ecology and Violence," *Criminology* 26 (1989): 553–89; William Julius Wilson, *The Truly Disadvantaged* (Chicago: University of Chicago Press, 1987).

9. Robert J. Sampson, "Crime in Cities: The Effects of Formal and Informal Social Control," in *Communities and Crime*, ed. Albert J. Reiss Jr. and Michael Tonry (Chicago: University of Chicago Press, 1986); Sampson and Groves, "Community Structure and Crime"; Robert J. Sampson, "Collective Regulation of Adolescent Misbehavior: Validation Results from Eighty Chicago Neighborhoods," *Journal of Adolescent Research* 12 (1997): 227–44.

10. Ruth Horowitz, "Community Tolerance of Gang Violence," *Social Problems* 34 (1987): 437–50; Colin Loftin and Robert H. Hill, "Regional Subculture and Homicide: An Examination of the Gastil-Hackney Thesis," *American Sociological Review* 39 (1974): 714–24; Robert Nash Parker and M. Dwayne Smith, "Deterrence, Poverty and Type of Homicide," *American Journal of Sociology* 85 (1979): 614–24; Wilson, *The Truly Disadvantaged*.

11. Albert Cohen, *Delinquent Boys* (Glencoe, IL: Free Press, 1955); Albert Sutherland, *The Sutherland Papers* (Bloomington: Indiana University Press, 1956);

Marvin Wolfgang and Franco Ferracuti, *The Subculture of Violence* (London: Tavistock, 1967).

12. Elijah Anderson, "The Code of the Streets," *The Atlantic Monthly* (May 1994): 81–94; Elijah Anderson, *The Code of the Street: Decency, Violence, and the Moral Life of the Inner City* (New York: W. W. Norton, 1999).

13. Derek Cornish, "Theories of Action in Criminology: Learning Theory and Rational Choice Approaches," in *Routine Activity and Rational Choice Advances in Criminological Theory*, Vol. 5, ed. Ronald V. Clarke and Marcus Felson (New Brunswick, NJ: Transaction Press, 1993); Jeffrey Fagan and Deanna L. Wilkinson, "Social Contexts and Functions of Adolescent Violence," in *Violence in American Schools: A New Perspective*, ed. Delbert S. Elliott and Beatrix A. Hamburg (New York: Cambridge University Press, 1998), 55–93; Richard B. Felson, "Predatory and Dispute-Related Violence: A Social Interactionist Approach," in *Routine Activity and Rational Choice, Advances in Criminological Theory*, Vol. 5, ed. Ronald V. Clarke and Marcus Felson (New Brunswick, NJ: Transaction Press, 1993), 103–25; Richard B. Felson and Henry J. Steadman, "Situational Factors in Disputes Leading to Criminal Violence," *Criminology* 21 (1983): 59–74; David F. Luckenbill and Danial P. Doyle, "Structural Position and Violence: Developing a Cultural Explanation," *Criminology* 27 (1989): 419–36; William Oliver, *The Violent Social World of Black Men* (New York: Lexington Books, 1994); Kenneth Polk, *When Men Kill: Scenarios of Masculine Violence* (New York: Cambridge University Press, 1994).

14. Anderson, "The Code of the Streets"; Geoffrey Canada, *Fist, Stick, Knife, Gun* (Boston: Beacon Press, 1995); Cornish, "Theories of Action in Criminology"; Fagan and Wilkinson, "Social Contexts and Functions of Adolescent Violence"; Jeffrey Fagan and Deanna L. Wilkinson, "Guns, Youth Violence, and Social Identity in Inner Cities," in *Youth Violence, Crime and Justice: A Review of Research*, vol. 24, ed. Michael Tonry (Chicago: University of Chicago Press, 1998), 105–88.

15. Cornish, "Theories of Action in Criminology"; Fagan and Wilkinson, "Social Contexts and Functions of Adolescent Violence"; Felson and Steadman, "Situational Factors"; David F. Luckenbill, "Criminal Homicide as a Situated Transaction," *Social Problems* 25 (1977): 176–86; Oliver, *The Violent Social World of Black Men*.

16. Anderson, "The Code of the Streets"; Fagan and Wilkinson, "Social Contexts and Functions of Adolescent Violence," and "Guns, Youth Violence."

17. Fagan and Wilkinson, "Social Contexts and Functions of Adolescent Violence."

18. The *Violence Prevention Network* is an initiative in the San Francisco Department of Health which is charged to work with a community steering committee to implement a violence prevention plan. *The Gangfree Communities Initiative* was a citywide effort to form a collaboration among city agencies and community-based organizations to implement a gang intervention model promoted by OJJDP (Office of Juvenile Justice and Delinquency Prevention of the U.S. Department of Justice) run out of the Mayor's Office on Criminal Justice (MOCJ). *Back on Track* is a project in the district attorney's office that diverts individuals who have been involved in the

juvenile justice system and have their first charged adult nonviolent offense. *BayView Magic* is a community collaboration for violence prevention in the BayView section of San Francisco which was developed and run out of the Public Defender's Office. *Community Connect* was the name of the failed community policing initiative located in SFPD (the San Francisco Police Department) and coordinated by MOCJ. *Safe Start* is an initiative that is attempting to reduce the incidence and impact of violence on San Francisco children ages birth to six years through collaboration between SFPD and CPS (Child Protective Services). *The Ceasefire Initiative* is the attempt of SFPD to replicate the Boston Ceasefire model. *Citysafe* is an approach to crime and violence reduction that coordinates the city's resources and focuses them on five broad areas: youth services, job creation, community development, criminal justice, and safer streets. *Communities of Opportunity* is a program in the Mayor's Office of Economic Development that utilizes community and public/private partnerships to target the five street corners in the city most impacted by violence with an integrated approach that includes physical improvements, intensive social services, and new employment opportunities.

19. William J. Chambliss, "Crime Control and Ethnic Minorities: Legitimizing Racial Oppression by Creating Moral Panics," in *Ethnicity, Race, and Crime: Perspectives Across Time and Place*, ed. Darnell F. Hawkins (Albany, NY: SUNY Press, 1995), 235–58.

20. N. Wallerstein and B. Duran, "The Conceptual, Historical and Practice Roots of Community Based Participatory Research and Related Participatory Traditions," in M. Minkler and N. Wallerstein, eds., *Community-Based Participatory Research for Health* (San Francisco: Jossey-Bass, 2003).

~

CHAPTER SIX

Private Troubles and Public Issues

Michael Burawoy

Perhaps the most widely cited and most celebrated words of any sociologist are those of C. Wright Mills when he defined the sociological imagination as the quality of mind that translates private troubles into public issues. The sociological imagination articulates individual experiences of unemployment, disease, murder, divorce, debt, poverty, and so forth as personal troubles. It then connects those personal troubles to the underlying wider social structures, thereby turning them into public issues for political contestation. What Mills fails to elaborate (what he leaves to the political imagination) is just how the transformation of private troubles into public issues takes place, who accomplishes it, and against what impediments it is accomplished.

The four case studies included in this volume (chapters 2, 3, 4, and 5) exemplify the sociological imagination—they link personal suffering to socially patterned inequalities in employment conditions, access to education, exposure to environmental hazards, and subjection to violence. But, more important, they exhibit a political imagination, that is, the political practice of turning personal distress into public issues. The contributors focus on the vehicles of such transformations, namely, the difficult and tension-ridden *chains of collaboration* linking university academics, the service professionals, and community activists to one another and to victimized populations. At the same time, they focus less on obstacles to *transforming common sense* that lie within the grip of an individual's psyche or the structure of lived experience.

At the other end of the collaborative chain, the studies also give short shrift to the *institutional obstacles* facing the organic intellectual, obstacles emanating from the university, the law firm, the community organization. I will deal with these three issues in turn—collaboration, common sense, and professional empowerment—but only after first considering the overall context that simultaneously demands and threatens the sociological imagination.

Privatization and Its Public Countermovements

As Andrew Barlow elaborates with such clarity in the Introduction, we are living in a period when the state no longer contains but promotes the excesses of the market economy. It has abandoned minimalist protection of its citizens against poverty and social insecurity in favor of tax incentives and lucrative contracts for corporations. The state is ever more hostile to policies that would reduce inequalities, limit the degradation of everyday life, and counteract exclusions and marginalizations. So, the advocates of social justice have had to turn away from the state as a site of struggle and direct attention to the disempowered communities themselves, seeking to rebuild civil society, even as it retreats. But this means a corresponding shift away from the top-down role of the traditional professionals who worked within the state on behalf of their clients and a shift toward an organic, direct connection of professionals and the communities whose needs and interests they defend.

One source of professionals is, of course, the university, but here too, changes are afoot, changes parallel to those in the state and redolent with implications for a public social science. After the eclipse of the wave of struggles for academic freedom at the end of the nineteenth and the beginning of the twentieth century, the hallmark of the American university has been its insulation from various publics. The disciplines that live within its walls are uniquely strong in protecting their professional autonomy. In recent years, however, those walls have become porous as the university has received offers it could not refuse, enticements from private corporations seeking to turn knowledge into profits, or from wealthy donors seeking tax shelters with ideological payoffs. As public universities receive an ever-smaller proportion of their revenues from the state, fees have increased by leaps and bounds, making the college degree a major financial investment.

There is, however, also a countermovement to the privatization of higher education, a countermovement that includes reaching out to communities of the poor and disadvantaged minorities. Even as it is being brought into the orbit of state and market, parts of the university community are wrestling themselves free to join forces with service professionals, also fleeing entrapment within the state. The case studies in this book exemplify this countermovement from private to public—projects that bring researchers, service professionals, and activists into an ongoing collaboration. Such exciting endeavors that extend rather than diminish the public role of the university and professions need to come out of the shade and into the limelight.

Chains of Collaboration

The organic relation between professionals and lower-class community is a two-way dialogue. It is based on a reciprocity that is hard to sustain as mutuality easily succumbs to domination. On the one hand, there is the danger of vanguardism in which professionals know best, imposing their learned theorizing on a recalcitrant community. On the other hand, professionals themselves can be captured by the communities they serve, or they can voluntarily bend over backwards to deny their autonomy, seeking full immersion. This is the danger of fadishism. What is striking about the four case studies is how they seek to avoid both pathologies and instead achieve a balanced mutuality that characterizes the organic relation.

One way to establish reciprocity is through the joint production of power. Professionals transmit their specialized knowledge—their cultural and social capital—to these communities, while the latter in turn mobilize what they have absorbed in order to advance their specific interests—to defend rights to respectful employment, education, and a healthy and safe environment. Although we don't hear directly from individuals who are members of the communities themselves (as all four chapters are written by the professionals) these are indeed presented as inspirational success stories. Anamaria Loya, in her moving rendition of the struggles of day laborers in San Francisco, shows how she transmits expertise and confidence to help them fight for their own rights, to be their own lawyers, to collectively organize against exploitative employers who might not even honor the simple wage contract. Michelle Renée, Jeannie Oakes, John Rogers, and Gary Blasi recount their efforts to work with community activists (advocates and organizers) to counter inequities in access to schooling. Manuel Pastor, Rachel Morello-Frosch, and James Sadd show how research identifies the unequal distribution of hazards from waste and toxic disposal facilities, helping communities hold public and private entities accountable to government regulations. Finally, Howard Pinderhughes argues for collaborative research that identifies the structural forces at work in promoting youth violence and the challenges of reversing those forces.

Successes these may be, but they are won in different ways. The collaboration between lawyers and day laborers involves transferring skills from professionals to community members, arming them with knowledge of their rights and with the collective organization to fight for those rights. Having grown up in a similar community of poor Hispanic laborers, Loya commands their confidence and conveys capital they didn't have before through the creation of a labor center. Howard Pinderhughes operates on an even deeper principle of immersion, compelling accountability to the community and voicing its needs to contain youth violence, often against misguided policies coming from outside. In both these cases, empowerment comes about through the merger of professional and activist.

In the other two cases presented in this volume, professional and activist maintain a certain separation. In the struggle against educational inequities, the professionals qua researchers are part of a university-based organization—IDEA (Institute for Democracy, Education, and Access)—and the activists are part of organizations (such as InnerCity Struggle, Parent U-Turn, and ACORN) that operate across communities. The researchers and activists collaborate under an umbrella organization, EJC (Education Justice Collaborative). The two-way collaboration does not rely so much upon self-imposed restraint or accountability on the part of the lone professional but upon institutional restraints. The chain of collaboration is held in reciprocal tension by the logic of organizations (IDEA, community organization, EJC). The same is true of the environmental justice movement. Here the researchers collaborated with activists in CBE (California's Communities for a Better Environment), but the collaboration was cultivated by Liberty Hill Foundation, which sought a sponsor of research (the California Endowment) that would demonstrate class and racial disparities in vulnerability to air pollution. This is so different from Pinderhughes, who is the lone activist-researcher immersed in a community.

Behind collaboration and reciprocity is the common endeavor to influence state policy or the distribution of resources. In this regard the professionals can help to increase the ability of communities to realize their interests and needs, by building their *mobilizing capacity* through, for example, the Day Laborers' Hiring Hall. Or professionals may act as mediators and interpreters to *legitimate, translate, and represent* demands of their community-based collaborators. With their social and cultural capital, professionals can give a particular type of public voice to demands for a more equitable access to education, or a reduction in environmental hazards or violence in poor communities, or the extension of rights for day laborers.

Empowerment involves not only endowing the community with the resources to fight for its interests but also disempowering institutions of domination. Of particular importance is the production and dissemination of science to counter the dominant ideologies that are part of the vehicles of oppression. Often, organic professionals find themselves arrayed against their professional colleagues on the other side of the fence. So Pinderhughes is unflagging in his opposition to "conventional" social science that would divide up the source of "problems" into a series of factors pointing to policy interventions (e.g., incarceration) that deepen rather than lessen violence. This piecemeal policy approach misses the overall context, failing to adopt a comprehensive approach necessary to bring amelioration.

The educational project of Michelle Renée and her colleagues began with a court case that sought to establish the State of California's responsibility for unequal distribution of educational resources. The State lost the case, and then the consortium of academics took on the role of overseeing implementation. Here, too, the academics had to fight a battle against state experts over the gathering and interpretation of data. Similarly in the case of the environmental justice movement, social scientists had to demonstrate that poor minority communities were at greater risk, which proved to be a major methodological dispute over units of analysis—zip codes versus census tracts. In other words, professionals can play an essential role in contesting hostile spokespersons of corporations and states, and this role becomes ever more important as the social justice agenda is publicly put on the defensive.

There was nothing preordained or "biased" about this research that sprung from contestation on behalf of social justice. Indeed, advocacy threw up unexpected discoveries—for example, that exposure to hazardous wastes peaked not with the poorest communities (who are removed from all economic activity) but in working-class communities of color. Yet, opponents of public social science often intimate that it is second rate, has lower standards. But the case studies presented here convincingly demonstrate not only the controversial character of so much public social science but the fact that because it is open to and subjected to public scrutiny and produced against great resistance means that it has to be of the highest quality. It has to withstand the assault of the paid servants of the dominant class and increasingly of the State. Poor research, no less than poor legal advocacy, will only bring defeat and disrepute to the cause of social justice.

Transforming Common Sense

Professional advocacy of social justice not only enhances mobilizing capacity, and not only contests dominant ideologies, but also elaborates, enriches, and sometimes even transforms the common sense. This dimension of empowerment rests on the assumption that oppressed peoples do not fully comprehend the conditions of their own subjugation. This is a hotly disputed issue within social science: that is, whether oppression leads to insight or false consciousness. There are those like Pierre Bourdieu who consider that subjugated groups driven by necessity cannot appreciate the nature and conditions of their subordination. Symbolic violence inures them to their subject status. On the other hand, feminists such as Patricia Hill Collins argue to the contrary, that insight comes from multiple oppressions—the more oppressed you are, the more transparent the subjugation.

I find myself between these extreme positions together with Marxists, such as Antonio Gramsci, who argue for a limited rather than a false consciousness, limited by the immediacy of oppression and the opportunity structures open to communities. When it comes to matters of social justice, for example, individuals may invest in strategies of social or geographical mobility, seeking to avoid toxic waste, violence, or poor schooling, rather than staying put and struggling for the community interest. Given the prevailing ideology and the remission of the welfare state, strategies of individual mobility are often preferred—based on unrealistic expectations—to collective mobilization. Thus, day laborers might prefer to operate independently from street corners and adopt a more competitive and entrepreneurial approach to finding jobs rather than rely on the more administered mechanisms of the Labor Center. Rather than demanding greater resources be put into education, poor people might see schooling as the avenue of mobility for their children or even themselves. Social science can present the depressing figures about the outcomes of social and geographical mobility for those with limited resources, but the turn to collective action is quite another matter. Tying private troubles to public issues cannot be effective without also convincing communities that collectively they can, for example, actually succeed in upgrading their local schools.

Recognizing social injustice is best accomplished by showing how some people are—for no good reason—much better off than others. It requires compelling comparisons among communities to reveal inequalities, which to some are obvious but to others remain obscure. Oppressed communities are often isolated, leading to exaggerations as well as underestimation of the differences along racial and class lines. Social science and law can bring into perspective the exploitation that lies behind personal suffering—how the advantages of a few create the disadvantage of the many, whether these disadvantages concern environmental hazards, education, housing, income, or whatever dimension may be experientially salient. Social science can also bear testimony to the mechanisms through which social inequality is reproduced and deepened—the effect of state withdrawal of funds for social protection and welfare leads the richest communities to exit state provisions and instead create, fund, and expand private schooling, hospitals, gated communities, and so forth with the result that public provision of such basic goods becomes even worse. Here the social scientist does not replace the experiential truth with a scientific truth but rather through collaboration with community members expands, deepens, and elaborates the experiential truth with the help of scientific research.

The supply of descriptions and explanations of social injustice can easily be disempowering if alternative approaches are not available. Conveying the problematic character of research models that lead to counterproductive piecemeal policy changes, while focusing on the broader, more enduring economic and political forces responsible for youth violence, can, paradoxically, paralyze a community. To know that one is at the bottom of the heap and that forces beyond one's control are responsible for keeping one there can lead to despair or self-defeating strategies of individual exit if the professional does not offer effective ways forward. In addition to elaborating the analytical powers of communities, the professional has to assume the critical role of working with advocates to supply alternatives. Anamaria Loya provides us with a most apt example of the hiring halls, which have grown up across the country to cater to the growing informal labor force outside the jurisdiction of labor unions. The same may be said of the organizing strategies of the SEIU (Service Employees International Union) that pioneered social movement unionism connecting workplace and community. From being the most difficult group to organize, immigrants became the group most receptive to new mobilization strategies that skirted the law, publicly humiliated employers, and enabled immigrant workers to put down roots not only in the workplace but also in the community. The union organizer first undertakes careful and detailed research into the weak links of a particular industry and then sets about exposing those links with innovative strategies worked out together with the community of affected workers.

A crucial part of the sociological imagination is the identification, articulation, and elaboration of alternative institutions or ways of organizing that spring up spontaneously in one locality or another. The social scientist then seeks to generalize their features, the conditions of existence, their weaknesses as well as their strengths. This is the utopian, or rather real utopian function of intellectuals, namely to imagine an institutional fabric that can supply the needs of poor communities directly or facilitate their capacity to struggle for those needs. No amount of critical analysis of neoliberalism, capitalist degradation, or state despotism can substitute for the institutional imagination necessary for forging an effective collective will. Indeed without this imagination for plausible alternatives, critique leads to cynicism and withdrawal.

Empowering the Professional

A public social science has three goals. The first is to empower subjugated communities in their relations to the structures of domination through collaborative relations between professionals and communities. The second goal is to transform common sense, turning private troubles into public issues. The third is to strengthen the legitimacy and power of the activist-professional and the public social scientist within the professional structures they inhabit.

While the intervention of the social scientist into the lived problems of poor communities generates new directions for research, the organization of the academy and the rhythm of the academic career are often at odds with that of the activist at work in the community. The academic has often considerable teaching and service commitments within the university and/or specific criteria for promotion and tenure that require academic publications in mainstream journals, all of which can be at odds with deep engagement with local struggles. Just as I noted at the beginning of this chapter that the policy world poses obstacles to the immediate realization of the interests of poor communities, so we may say the same of the professional world that expects research to be accountable to peers rather than subjects, to be accessible to a narrow range of specialists rather than a lay audience, and to answer the puzzles of scientific research programs rather than be relevant to public issues. These are real contradictions that coexist alongside the synergies described in the four projects that make up this volume.

Still, there are always spaces within the modern university to develop and practice a range of forms of public engagement. Indeed, teaching itself can be seen as one of those public engagements. At the same time, however, we should not think of the university as a homogeneous environment. Within the university there is a powerful ranking of different schools (professional versus academic), and even within schools there is often a strong balkanization of disciplines. Across the complex system of American higher education, we find a steeply hierarchical system ranging from high-flying research universities with internationally known faculty to two-year colleges and their often dedicated teachers. One might argue, and there is much evidence for this, that the lower tiers of tertiary education are more organically tied to dispossessed communities while the upper tiers are more likely to follow traditional patterns of influence whether through media or policy research.

Here an old distinction, drawn from sociology, between locals and cosmopolitans is useful. Conventionally, social science has striven for theories or laws that have universal applicability, that are applicable irrespective of social and historical context. Even when the locality is studied, as in some of the most famous works of social science, the objective is to arrive at results that transcend or repress the context. Thus in the field of sociology, when Arlie Hochschild writes of the domestic division of labor in *The Second Shift* or Robert Bellah and his colleagues write of individualism in *The Habits of the Heart,* their accounts refer to all America, even though the material they gathered comes from interviews in specific places in California. In their cosmopolitan ambition they lose sight of the local upon which their generalizations rest.

The development of organic relations between social scientist and community, a relationship of mutual accountability and reciprocity, calls for the valorization of the local relationship. It calls for a vision of social science that builds up from the particularity to the general, to see the particular not as an instance of the general but as something determined and shaped by broader social forces in which it is embedded. The relation between community and context is the object of analysis when Mitchell Duneier studies the sidewalks of Greenwich Village or Loïc Wacquant studies the boxing gym in South Chicago. Their cosmopolitan reach is built on case studies that are explicitly understood to be local. This public ethnography can incorporate the organic relation between social scientist and community.

All four case studies in this volume are first and foremost local; they are responsive to the needs of communities in California. They are building toward a public social science that is not simply *in* California but also *for* California. Moreover, they have a pedigree that includes such eminent investigators as Cary McWilliams, Paul Taylor, Clerk Kerr, and Mike Davis. But we cannot stop here. California, after all, is at the crossroads of the world, of North and South, East and West, so that the local studies of environment, education, violence, and labor when put in their global context tell us a great deal about processes taking place in many parts of the world. Just as Mills spoke of turning private troubles into public issues, today we must speak of turning local problems into global issues. The empowerment of the organic intellectuals, whether they are lawyers or academics, must come through their collaboration in a common project of building a public vision that is local in its roots but global in scope.

~

About the Contributors

Andrew Barlow teaches sociology at Diablo Valley College and the University of California at Berkeley. He is the author of *Between Fear and Hope: Globalization and Race in the United States*. A longtime civil rights activist, Dr. Barlow has participated in the campaigns to prevent passage of anti–civil rights ballot initiatives in California. He coauthored an amicus brief in a school integration case before the U.S. Supreme Court and has testified as an expert witness in race discrimination cases in California courts. Barlow is on the board of directors of La Raza Centro Legal in San Francisco.

Gary Blasi joined the UCLA law faculty with a distinguished twenty-year record of public interest practice. He specializes in advocacy on behalf of children in substandard schools, homeless families and individuals, low-income tenants, low-wage workers, and victims of discrimination. He also serves as the acting director of the UCLA Institute of Industrial Relations, which supports research and education on issues critical to working people.

Michael Burawoy teaches sociology at the University of California at Berkeley. After many years of participating in and studying industrial workplaces with a view to changing sociology, he is now studying the academic workplace in order to understand how sociology can further the transformation of society. With this end in mind he has promoted public sociologies in all corners of the globe—public sociologies that bring sociologists into dialogue with diverse publics, thereby linking private troubles to political issues, a precondition for the success of projects for social justice. Burawoy was president of the American Sociological Association in 2004.

Anamaria Loya is executive director of La Raza Centro Legal in San Francisco, a Latino community organization that combines legal advocacy with community organizing and leadership training and development.

Rachel Morello-Frosch is the Carney Assistant Professor of Environmental Studies and the Department of Community Health at Brown University Medical School. She has published widely on environmental justice and environmental health inequalities. She is also the cofounder of the Environmental Leadership Program, a nationally renowned two-year fellowship program and nonprofit center for environmental leadership and professional development, and she sits on the scientific advisory board of Breast Cancer Action in San Francisco.

Jeannie Oakes is Presidential Professor in Educational Equity and director of UCLA's Institute for Democracy, Education, and Access (IDEA) and the University of California's All Campus Consortium on Research for Diversity (ACCORD). Oakes's research focuses on schooling inequalities and follows the progress of educators and activists seeking socially just schools. Oakes and John Rogers are coauthors of *Learning Power: Organizing for Education and Justice* (Teachers College Press, 2006), which reports on students, parents, teachers, and grassroots groups struggling for more socially just schools.

Manuel Pastor is Professor of Geography and American Studies and Ethnicity at the University of Southern California (USC). His research has generally focused on the labor market and social conditions facing low-income urban communities; his most recent book, coauthored with Chris Benner and Laura Leete, is *Staircases or Treadmills: Labor Market Intermediaries and Economic Opportunity in a Changing Economy* (Russell Sage, 2007). He has a long history of collaboration with environmental and social justice organizations on a variety of research and policy efforts such as efforts to promote environmental integrity, living wages, and more equitable development.

Howard Pinderhughes is Associate Professor and Chair of the Department of Social and Behavioral Sciences at the University of California, San Francisco. He is the author of *Race in the Hood: Conflict and Violence Among Urban Youth*, a study of racial attitudes and racial violence among youth in New York City. Dr. Pinderhughes has worked for the last fifteen years with community-based organizations and schools in San Francisco's Mission District and Bay View Hunter's Point neighborhoods, conducting community-based research on youth violence, gang violence, and adolescent relationship violence, as well as providing training, workshops, and assistance in program development in the areas of adolescent violence prevention and intervention and race relations among youth.

Michelle Renée is a postdoctoral fellow at UCLA's Institute for Democracy Education, and Access. Her dissertation, *Knowledge, Power and Education Justice: How Social Movement Organizations Use Research to Influence Education Policy*, investigated the increased activism of education justice organizations that represent low-income communities and communities of color in the California education policy process. Prior to entering academe, Dr. Renée worked as a legislative assistant in the U.S. Congress. She has her roots in student organizing and was one of the cofounders of the Sierra Student Coalition (the student arm of the Sierra Club) and has been a part of numerous community organizations.

John Rogers is an Assistant Professor in UCLA's Graduate School of Education and Information Studies and the Co-Director of UCLA's Institute for Democracy, Education, and Access (IDEA). Rogers studies strategies for engaging urban youth, community members, and educators in equity-focused school reform. Since 1999, Rogers has led a summer seminar for urban youth in critical sociology. He also has directed a seminar in participatory research for members of grassroots community groups. Rogers is co-author (with Jeannie Oakes) of *Learning Power: Organizing for Education and Justice*.

James L. Sadd is Professor of Environmental Science at Occidental College in Los Angeles. His research interests and experience include spatial analysis and digital mapping using geographic information systems (GIS) and image analysis software and are focused on quantitative analysis of environmental justice issues. He is active in environmental justice issues in the southern California area, presently serving as a member of the Green LA Cumulative Impacts Working Group, providing recommendations to the office of the Mayor of Los Angeles to support his efforts to improve health in low-income communities of color.